LOVED UNCONDITIONALLY

A Spiritual Memoir of Trauma, Addiction Recovery, and Finding God Beyond Religion

FENIX SHEPHARD

ISBN Paperback: 979-8-9958342-1-2
ISBN Electronic: 979-8-9958342-0-5

Library of Congress Control Number: 2026910684

Publishing Consultant: PRESStinely - PRESStinely.com

Portions of this book are works of nonfiction.
Certain names and identifying characteristics have been changed.

Printed in Houston, Texas, United States of America.

Fenix Shepard
The Unconventional Counselor
FenixShepard.com

DISCLAIMER

Dedication

To God — my Abba, my Father, my Love. You never left. Not once. This book is Yours.

To Marlee — my service dog, my soul mate, my greatest teacher of unconditional love. You were two weeks old, found in a dumpster, sick and fighting for your life. I thank God that He blessed me with you.

To Mom and Dad — God restored what time had separated. I am grateful for every moment we have now. I love you more than words on a page can hold.

And to every searching soul and every wounded spirit who was handed shame before they were ever handed love — this book was written for you. You are why I survived. You are why I told the truth. You are why every word on every page exists.

You are loved. Unconditionally. Always.
— Fenix

Foreword

There are books that teach you something. And then there are books that change you.
Unconditional is the second kind.

When Fenix first stepped into my world, I saw something in her that many people miss in themselves — strength wrapped in sensitivity, courage hiding behind survival, and a voice that had not yet fully claimed its power.

What you are about to read is not theory. It is not curated inspiration. It is not a polished, filtered version of pain.

It is truth.

And truth, when spoken bravely, is medicine.

As a coach, I have worked with thousands of individuals learning to find their voice, refine their message, and stand confidently in their story. But the ones who truly transform are not the ones who memorize scripts. They are the ones who decide to stop hiding.

Fenix made that decision.

This book is raw because healing is raw. It is real because growth is real. It is uncomfortable in places because transformation requires honesty.

What moves me most is not simply that she survived her journey. It is that she chose to make meaning from it. She chose to take experiences that could have hardened her and instead allow them to deepen her compassion.

That is leadership.

We live in a world that rewards performance and perfection. *Unconditional* dares to offer something far more powerful — authenticity. It reminds us that healing doesn't come from pretending we're fine. It comes from remembering who we are beneath the wounds.

Fenix does not position herself above you in these pages. She walks beside you. She opens doors she once had to force open herself. She hands you a flashlight and says, "You're not alone in this."

That takes extraordinary courage.

As her coach, I have witnessed her evolution — from questioning her worth to claiming it, from shrinking her voice to honoring it. This book is not just a memoir. It is evidence. Evidence that when you decide to confront your truth instead of outrun it, something powerful happens.

You reclaim yourself.

If you are holding this book, I believe it is not by accident. There is something in these pages meant to meet you exactly where you are.

Read it slowly. Let it challenge you. Let it soften you. Let it remind you.

Healing is not about becoming someone new. It is about returning to who you have always been — unconditionally.

And Fenix Shepard has given you a brave map back to yourself.

— Dr. Forbes Riley

Table of Contents

Foreword v

Introduction: Who I Am and Why I Wrote This Book.............ix

Chapter 1: Leaving Innocence Behind 1

Chapter 2: Answering the Call..9

Chapter 3: Releasing First Love 21

Chapter 4: Surrendering to Heal......................................33

Chapter 5: Letting Go 41

Chapter 6: Seeing Signs from Beyond..............................49

Chapter 7: Missing the Mark..55

Chapter 8: Hearing the Voice 65

Chapter 9: Honoring Love 73

Chapter 10: God Provides 83

Chapter 11: Becoming Christlike 95

Chapter 12: God in the Cabin...105

Chapter 13: What God Showed Me About the Cross 115

Chapter 14: Love Even After Rejection............................121

Chapter 15: What Is Christ Consciousness? 129

Chapter 16: Trusting the Journey 139

Chapter 17: Awakening the Christ Within 147

Chapter 18: Healing Every Layer......................................155

Chapter 19: Building Sacred Partnership..........................163

Chapter 20: Following God's Voice Within 167

Chapter 21: Your Call to Awakening 173

Epilogue...177

Afterword: The Way Shower...................................179

Meet the Author...181

Who I Am and Why I Wrote This Book

I wrote this book to share how embracing Christ consciousness —
living rooted at the frequency of unconditional love — transformed
my life. Christ consciousness is living from the heart, not the ego.
It does not replace Jesus Christ, and it has little to do with religion.
It is an awakening — realizing Christ's divinity and oneness in all
of humanity. When you remember this for yourself, your whole
mind shifts into a deeper consciousness, and you experience inner
peace — always, naturally.

This is not only a book for the LGBTQ+ community — though I
pray it brings deep healing to every queer person who reads it. This
is a book for every human being who has ever felt too broken, too
ashamed, or too far outside the lines to be loved by God. It is for
the veteran. The addict. The abuse survivor. The divorced person.
The one who left the church wounded. The one who never found
their way in. The one who is lying awake right now wondering if
their life has any meaning at all. If any part of that is you — keep
reading. This book was written for you.

For many years, I struggled with trauma, addiction, and mental
health challenges. My journey was marked by anger, bitterness,
and a sense of being lost. However, a profound spiritual experience
— not through religion or another person, but through a direct
encounter with God — began my healing. I was then able to see
that God was with me all along. I just needed to reach out to Him.

This narrative begins with suffering, but it is ultimately a story of transformation and hope. As someone who was born gay and faced rejection and misunderstanding within religious spaces, I believe my experiences offer a unique perspective on the heart of God and Christ — unconditional love. My intention is to guide all readers, from all walks of life — straight, gay, those suffering from mental illness or addiction — toward inner healing and self-acceptance, regardless of their background or beliefs. I do use Scripture to share my perspective, as it is my desire to help as many people heal from religious trauma, or what others call "church hurt." This story is not for one type of person — it is for all people who are searching for meaning and longing to discover God's love, grace, and acceptance, regardless of their circumstances. I promise that this story will show you how God works in anyone's life, regardless of who they are or what they have done.

— Fenix Shepard

First, there was suffering . . .

A Moment for Reflection

Before you begin, ask yourself — what is the one wound you have been carrying the longest, and what would your life look like if you finally set it down?

Chapter 1

Leaving Innocence Behind

I'm fourteen years old, eyes wide open, lying in bed at 5:59 a.m., watching the clock, waiting for it to turn to 6:00. I've mustered the courage to leave home. Jermel is on his way to take me to my gay friend Daniel's house to live. I'm in high school and getting ready to act like a grown-up. You see, a month prior, I'd written a love letter to a girl I'd been walking home from school with, and I'd gathered the pluck to say, "I want you to be my girlfriend."

She wasn't into girls. She gave my letter to her father. Our home phone rang. My father picked it up — it was the girl's dad. He wasn't upset, just concerned, and asked Dad to address the issue.

Dad hung up, called my siblings Jane and Tom to the kitchen table, and then called me. He sat at the end of the table with my siblings across from me. Infuriated, embarrassed, and disgusted, he balled up his fist, slammed it down, and he looked at me and said.

"Are you a sicko lesbian?"

My heart sank. "No, Dad, I'm not a lesbian."

I looked at my siblings. They looked sorrowful, watching me be humiliated for not even understanding that I was gay. A few days later, I decided to end my life. I grabbed a bottle of Tylenol and a bottle of ibuprofen and swallowed a handful — about sixty-plus pills — and then went about my day as if nothing was wrong.

Four hours later, I showered, put on my pajamas, and put myself to bed. I would never have to wake up and feel this way again: disgusting, like something was seriously wrong with me. At 11:00 p.m., I woke up, ready to vomit. As I lay curled around the toilet, pale and heaving, Mom burst into the bathroom.

"Hija, what have you done?"

I couldn't speak. I was vomiting.

Mom dragged me up, shoved me into the car, and rushed me to the hospital. I choked down liquid charcoal so I could stop retching. The doctor called the police.

An older officer hustled into my room, thrust a flashlight in my face, and growled, "Where d'ya get the cocaine?" I stared at him with confusion and fear. I didn't know police officers were so aggressive to little children. The drug test showed I'd done cocaine. For the next twenty-four hours, I couldn't even sip water. If I did, I'd throw up.

After I was released from the hospital, Mom drove me home, and I crawled into bed. *Why didn't I die?*

The following week, I saw Dad clean his gun. He put it in his nightstand, loaded. After school, I grabbed the gun, put it underneath my tee shirt, and tiptoed to my room. I turned on R&B music, got on my knees, and snatched up a pillow. *This is it.* I pulled the trigger. Nothing.

Never having held a gun, I didn't know about the safety switch. While I was figuring it out, Jane opened my door, screamed, and ran to call Mom. Mom stood at my bedroom door and said, "If you're going to kill yourself, do it outside. I don't want blood on my carpet." She huffed away and called the police. I was admitted to the hospital after attempting suicide. A week after I was released, I realized — *I need to leave home.*

6:00 a.m. I got dressed and yanked my clothes from the closet. At 6:30, Jermel arrived, and as I was walking out of the house with a heap of clothes in my arms, Mom and Dad woke up. Dad stood at their bedroom door in a tee shirt and sweats. Mom stood next to him, arms folded, face grim. Dad snipped, "Are you leaving?"

I said nothing.

My parents stood there, and I realized they thought leaving would be the best decision for our family. They went back into their bedroom, shut the door, and let me walk out. I was fourteen.

After leaving my childhood home, I jumped into Jermel's car, and my early teenage years flashed through my mind. Back in Mexico City when I was six, Mom and Dad really never had my back. They had pretty much ignored me, and I'm guessing they knew about the abuse I suffered at the hands of people I didn't know. I had played with my neighbor — a grown man who took advantage of my trust and innocence. Then a distant cousin came to stay. She slept in my bed and fondled me.

Predatory behavior seemed to run in the family. When I was twelve, everyone knew that Grandpa was touching young girls. Grandma turned a blind eye. One morning, after I had spent the night with my grandparents, I crawled into bed with Grandma to cuddle. When she got up to shower, Grandpa stayed in bed. Once he heard the running water, he rolled over on top of me and rubbed himself against me.

Because I had experienced sexual abuse at such a young age, I displayed behaviors that were not normal for a little girl — touching my private parts in public constantly. Mom and I both knew that was unhealthy, but she didn't know how to help me. So when Dad called me a "sicko lesbian," I was already ashamed. *Why was I acting the way I did?*

Leaving home was — or so I thought — in my best interest.

At fifteen, I was working full time as a cook at a burger joint, attending high school, and moving around a lot. I was couch surfing, but somehow I was being protected, and I kept my head above water. But when a high school buddy gave me a stolen ID that belonged to a woman of drinking age, I let loose! I'd go to gay bars and drink and dance the night away. I was having girlfriends and having sex, but keeping it together — well, as much as a teenager could.

I believed that staying in school would show my parents that I loved them. When it was time to graduate high school, at almost eighteen years old, I called Dad. "Hey, Dad, I am graduating. Will you guys come?"

"Will your girlfriend be there?" he asked.

"Yes."

"Then we won't be coming."

I walked across the stage alone. It was heartbreaking. They couldn't love me just for being their child.

When we were both eighteen, Daniel's parents kicked him out because he was gay. So we got an apartment together. We were two abandoned kids living together, holding each other up. It was my safe zone, but still, I was losing at love and losing my life to booze. I was poor and scrounged for pennies so I could buy ramen noodles. I wandered the aisles of big box stores just to stay cool in the AC during the hot Fresno summers. The furniture I contributed to our space came from the dumpster, and for two months I had no mattress and slept on the floor. But when I got a used, stained, twin-size mattress, it was like heaven.

When I was nineteen years old, I met a new friend, Michelle, who introduced me to meth. No one told me that doing drugs would create even more havoc in my life. I hated it, but I still craved it. It made me feel nothing. I was snorting meth every day at work and every night at home. I couldn't sleep. It was exhausting. My girlfriend cheated on me, and that heartbreak shattered me. Curled up in the fetal position on my stained mattress, sobbing, I realized: *I need to leave. I need a fresh start. I'm moving to Long Beach. I'm getting away from all of this.* And I did.

I found a place with a roommate — a flashy bombshell named Jessica. When I got a job, I thought things would go better for me. But my manager harassed me sexually, and once I reported him, I was fired. I felt like I had a sign on my forehead: "Harass me." Absolute strangers would violate my personal space and get away with it. Why? Because I would freeze — just like that little girl in bed with Grandpa. *What's wrong with me?*

Lacking the support of loved ones or the guidance of my parents, I found comfort in my friends. But my judgment was impaired, and I attracted drug addicts. I met Clara at a job. She was a stay-at-home lesbian mom in a committed relationship. She bowled me over with her kind, loving ways. But she was a drug user. One day, she came to my apartment and said, "Hey, wanna party?" She grabbed a light bulb from a lamp, cracked it, put meth inside, put a straw in the bulb, lit the powder, and inhaled. And that's how I learned to smoke meth.

So there I was — now twenty-one, cracked out on drugs, and still drinking heavily. I saw people losing their minds, losing control of their bodies, and doing things they would normally never do. I let drug dealers use my car to transport drugs while being surveilled by drug enforcement officers. It could have landed me in prison. What I got out of it was free drugs. Still, being a hard worker, I knew I had to keep working to support my lifestyle. I was exhibiting post-traumatic stress symptoms and anxiety. Angry, sad, and depressed, I used substances to cope with my illness and broken heart. Time and time again, I looked at myself in the mirror, sobbing, "Fenix. You know you don't want to be doing this. What's happening to you?"

I came to my senses and tried to stop using. I was on and off the wagon when I met Alyssa. She was tall, beautiful, smart, and funny. I fell in love with her immediately — and, lucky me, she fell in love with me too. We moved in together and had a wild love affair, but my fear of abandonment kicked in. The best thing to do, I decided, was to smoke meth and escape the fact that one day Alyssa would stop loving me and leave.

One night, Alyssa and I were arguing, and I left our apartment to take a walk and regroup. It was around 11:30 p.m. There was a light misty rain. I was wearing a ball cap, a leather jacket, and jeans. I walked to the ocean but stayed above the beach, where there was a grassy area with cement tables and benches, across from a line of beachfront homes. I found a bench and sat down. I could see a vista of stars, the moon, and the ocean. I prayed for the first time. "God, if you can hear me, please help me."

Boy, was my prayer answered.

I heard a vehicle pull up and park close to where I was sitting. I looked back and saw, in a silver two-door car, a man staring straight ahead — serious, wearing eyeglasses and a white-collared shirt.

When I looked away, I heard a voice: "You're in danger. Get up." For a second, I thought nothing of it. Again the voice said, "You're in danger. Get up."

Something's wrong. I need to get home.

The man started his engine, did a U-turn, and parked in the direction I was walking. I turned around and walked the other way. He drove, parked next to me, and opened his door. I ran across the street toward a row of beach houses.

He shut his car door and drove around the block. I was shaking with fear — I was being hunted. I hid, ducking down behind cars, still running, watching for him as he was looking for me. It was midnight and very dark. I needed help. *Knock on doors*, I told myself. I whispered, "Why would someone open the door for me?" I rang a doorbell. No answer. I hid.

Where was he? I saw him driving past. I ran to the next house and rang the doorbell. No answer. But the house had a tall ceramic flowerpot. I squatted behind it and prayed, "God, if this is you, please help me."

The voice said, "Get up. Run. Run across the street." Terrified, I got up and ran as fast as I could — crossing the yard, crossing the sidewalk, seeing nothing but open space for this man to find me, capture me. But when my foot touched the sidewalk on the other side of the street, an older man appeared out of nowhere, holding his bike. He looked to be in his late sixties. I yelled out, "Please help me!" I grabbed his arms, trying to catch my breath, and pointed. "That man is chasing me. He's trying to catch me!"

The man said, "You're safe. I'm here." As soon as he said this, the predator turned the corner. We locked eyes. I pointed. "That's the guy who's chasing me!"

The predator took off. On that night, he did not catch his prey.

The man with the bike walked with me all the way home. The funny thing is, I remember him saying, "All I remember is that I was at home. I don't remember when I started walking my bike out this late at night." I believe he was an angel — sent to protect me from whatever that predator had planned.

I would love to tell you that after that night things got better for me. But they didn't. At twenty-three, my meth addiction was raging. I was trading sex for drugs and cheating on Alyssa. I hated who I'd become, and because I didn't love myself, how in the world could I love another person?

The truth is, we can't love someone when we're lost to addiction. The fights with Alyssa got so bad we started fist-fighting. Then I did something terrible, something shameful — and she hates me to this day. We had a joint bank account. I knew she was about to leave me, so before she could, I closed the account and took the $24,000. The next day, she noticed the account had been closed. That night, I threw the first punch, and we fought. I had to leave before she called the cops. I would have been arrested.

We never spoke again.

> **A Moment for Reflection**
> Have you ever been shamed for who you are at the very moment you were just beginning to understand yourself?

Chapter 2

Answering the Call

Alyssa's $24,000 was going to buy me a future. I invested with two chefs-turned-drug-dealers to buy $5,000 worth of ecstasy to resell. After I gave my "colleagues" the money, they quit the restaurant and took off with the cash. Talk about instant karma. I had to take a good look at myself — it was six months before my twenty-fourth birthday. I was still using meth, still an alcoholic, still broke, still making bad decisions, still suffering from mental illness. Even though I was hardworking, my sassy attitude made my employers want to fire me, so before they could, I'd already have another job lined up.

On the night of September 10, 2001, I visited Tom. We drank the night away happily. At 10:00 a.m. on September 11, I opened my eyes — head spinning, mouth dry, needing to pee, and needing coffee and food. I got up and drove my hungover self to get breakfast fixings and coffee. I sat on the couch and turned on the television, and watched, horrified, as the Twin Towers fell. *Are we at war?*

That same week, I visited my parents. Even though we were estranged, I wanted to see them. I treated them with respect, but I couldn't keep my hands out of their liquor cabinet — by the time I left, the cabinet was bereft of booze. I was still grieving Alyssa. I wanted to change my life. Surely it had more to offer than this miserable, lonesome, dejected, drug-addicted lifestyle. I wanted more.

I needed a job and a place to live, so I took a risk and stayed with Mom and Dad in Fresno. When I put "cooking jobs in Fresno" into an online search bar and pressed Enter, the page redirected to the

United States Navy. The words "Come Join the United States Navy" were superimposed over the image of an aircraft carrier. I stared and thought, *I won't be accepted. I have a past.* I navigated away from the page and continued my search. That same week, I had an interview for a cooking position downtown, and as I was driving to the appointment, I stopped at a traffic light. I looked up and saw a billboard: "Come Join the United States Navy." I stared at it until the light turned green. I took that job downtown — although I really didn't want it. One afternoon, I took a different route home to my parents' place, and at a stoplight I looked to my left and saw a Navy Recruiting building. I made a U-turn and parked.

Should I go inside? Should I reveal my drug history? I said out loud, "Just go inside and ask questions." I marched through the heavy double doors and found myself face to face with a six-foot, five-inch soldier who greeted me warmly and shook my hand. He taught me how to salute and told me I'd be a great addition to the United States Navy. I left exhilarated and positive. *This is what I want to do with my life!* That week, I signed up for the Navy.

Because of September 11, I was scheduled to leave Fresno for medical qualifications within two weeks — then off to boot camp in Chicago. I finally had structure and discipline in my life.

I loved boot camp. This was the first time I felt part of something bigger than myself.

Six months into my service, I was given orders to join my first ship. I was flown in a military helicopter to the Middle East to meet the ship. I stayed in a hotel with a guard at my door. I had a week to walk around and take in the sights, and I learned the hard way that I ought to have been wearing a hijab. I escaped that situation unscathed and was then helicoptered to the ship. Within an hour of being aboard, I was sexually harassed. Clearly the sign "Harass Me" was plastered invisibly across my forehead. My full-day escort and welcome host — a less-than-honorable sailor named James — took me to a part of the ship that was unnecessary to see unless there were other motives. His intentions were obvious. I froze like the little girl in Mexico City. Word spread quickly: "The new recruit is someone we can touch inappropriately." Other sailors did the same — and each time, I froze.

One day, I met a sailor named Jonathan. He seemed friendly — no sexual advances. He sent me an email on the military system: "It was really nice to meet you. Maybe you and I can go hang out when we make it to port?" I was new and wanted to make friends. "That would be nice," I emailed back. I had no intention of dating him, just building rapport with fellow sailors I would spend the next three years with. But Jonathan's intentions were malicious. When the ship docked on a beautiful island, Jonathan made his move. He found me standing on deck watching the seamen tie us to the dock.

"Fenix. I've got a room for us. I will see you out there tonight."

"What?" I was scared and angry. I'd already been dealing with men in the engine room showing me their bodies and touching me — as if any of that was normal. I told myself to find safe friends to spend the night with. I found a fellow sailor named Christie. "Can I tag along with you?" "Sure," she said. Our group was three women and one man — Tony. We got dressed, went to a seafood restaurant, had incredible food, and drank delicious wine. We had so much fun. I felt safe and was enjoying getting to know these people. Later in the evening, the energy shifted. We were nightclubbing, and I allowed myself to drink tequila shots. My night of fun would quickly become a nightmare.

The other two women went back to the ship, while Tony and I went across the street to another nightclub. I felt very drunk. I sat down, and my head spun.

Tony saw I was in distress and said, "I left my sweater at the other club. Stay here — I'll run and get it and come back. We'll head back to the ship."

The moment he left, I realized Jonathan was in the club. He walked up and said, "You know you're in a restricted club? You need to come with me." Because he was a first-class petty officer and my superior, I listened to him. I stood up and blacked out. I have no memory of exiting that club, no memory of going to a hotel. But I remember being raped all night by him.

When I woke up, I was in a hotel room — naked, ashamed, confused, and angry. I sat slumped at the edge of the bed, holding my pounding head. "What did you do?" I wailed. "I didn't want to sleep with you! I'm going to report you."

"You'll be called a slut," he said, unfazed. He sauntered across the room and tossed my clothes at me. "Get dressed. They might slap me on the wrist, but this will be on you." He knew he would get away with it. "Let it go."

He was right — at least about how it would be handled. I reported him anyway, and the next day I was given a first-class ticket on a private jet all the way home to the United States. The Navy abandoned me. No support, no follow-up, nothing. When I arrived home, I hired a military attorney — a JAG lawyer — to help fight my case.

I drank my life away. I felt like I was only good for one thing — allowing men to use my body for their pleasure. I hated my life, and I hated being alive.

Even though I was already suffering enormously from addiction and pain, a greater force — God — was keeping me safe and sustaining me with grace and mercy. Every betrayal, every injustice I had to endure was making me unbreakable.

For the next two years, I waited for the trial against Jonathan. I wasn't allowed to continue my deployment or transfer to another naval station. I was given orders to work in the Chaplain's office. It was my saving grace — assisting the Chaplain Chief and Officers. One day, they sent me home early so I could come back to help with a monthly military wives' meeting. I went in an hour early to make sure everything was set up. One chaplain was still there.

"Sir, you're still here?"

He looked up. "Hi there. Yes, I stayed and read this book about Jesus." He smiled, his eyes twinkling. "Do you know Jesus?"

"A little," I said. I gestured toward the painting of Christ on the cross. "Something about dying on the cross."

"Sit down," the Chaplain said, motioning to a chair. "Why are you here? Tell me about your life."

I sat down. "Well," I said, "unfortunately, I was recently raped. I was flown off the ship after reporting it. Now I'm here."

He stood up, grabbed a chair, set it in front of me, and sat down. "I'm so sorry. I'm Father Benedict. Please — tell me more."

I told him I'd been living on my own since I was fourteen, struggling to survive. All I understood about life was that it was about suffering and pain. I didn't see a reason to live, but since I was here, I would try to make the best of what I was given. I could see it hurt him to hear about someone suffering for so long — with no parental guidance, no one to love them, and no one to protect them.

He was such a kind man. "Let me tell you about Jesus," he said.

That night, I heard about who Jesus was and learned what He had done for humanity. Like me, Jesus had suffered — but through His pain, He became a light for humankind.

Father Benedict leaned in and said, "Will you give your life to Jesus?"

With tears falling down my face, I said, "I will."

"Let me pray over you before these ladies arrive." Father Benedict stood up, put his hands on my head, and looked skyward.

As he prayed for me, I wept softly. I felt the grace of the Divine descend upon me. Then a dozen well-dressed ladies arrived, chattering, giggling, and gossiping, and I rose to greet them. "Thank you, Father," I whispered.

There was such joy in that room that night. The ladies were friendly, and we all had fun together. I was able to open up and talk — to really be myself. After I closed the hall for the evening, I walked to the barracks singing. I felt better than I had in years.

The next morning, I left for Boston. There was a woman there I had met online, and I was ready for love and affection. I was looking forward to being with my kind.

Being gay wasn't something people talked about openly yet. The only way I could meet another woman was in an online chat room. I had befriended Julie, and she had invited me to visit her in Boston. I wanted privacy, as there was still a "Don't Ask, Don't Tell" policy that would get gay and lesbian service members kicked out with a dishonorable discharge. I hopped in my SUV and drove all night along the East Coast. I arrived at Julie's apartment at 3:00 a.m. "Come in, Fenix," she said. "I have a room for you."

After a couple of hours of sleep, I came downstairs, met her family, and we had a late breakfast. Then everyone went about their day. I was sitting at the table drinking coffee when I heard the familiar voice say, "You're in danger." My ears perked up. I put my coffee down and had a sudden urge to leave. I said to Julie, "Something's wrong. I need to leave."

Confused, she said, "Okay. Do what you need to do."

I grabbed my bag, jumped in my SUV, and headed back toward base — twelve hours away. I didn't know what was wrong. All I knew was that the voice had saved my life once before, and I would trust it again.

I drove six hours without stopping for gas, food, or to use the restroom. Night fell, and the weather changed dramatically. Snow was falling fast, the temperature dropped, and the road got slippery. My windshield was frozen with ice — I could barely see. This was my first time driving in these conditions. I was headed for the George Washington Bridge. I turned off my radio. I needed to pray. "God, were you the one who told me I was in danger? Why does it feel like you led me into danger?"

God said, *"Go over the George Washington Bridge, and there you will find shelter."*

Upset, scared, and uncomfortable — driving on the freeway at five miles an hour, leaning over the steering wheel and peering out the windshield, blinded by snow — I said out loud, "God, why did you put me in danger like this?" I took the next exit. Regardless of what God had just said to me, I realized I didn't trust His voice. I pulled over and prayed. "God, I'm asking you — please find me a place to lay my head. It's so dark, and I'm so scared of driving in this weather. I'm freezing!"

After that quick prayer, I pulled back onto the road and drove a few blocks. A gas station was open, and when I pulled in, I saw a police car. After filling my tank, I walked over to the police vehicle, held up my military ID, and said, "Good evening. I'm looking for a hotel near here. Can you help me?"

One officer said, "You need to drive back onto the freeway and go over the George Washington Bridge. You'll find several hotels after you pay your bridge toll. If you want, we can lead the way. Follow us, and we'll get you back onto the freeway." I followed them to the bridge on-ramp. They pulled over, rolled down their window, and one of them said, "Go up the ramp and keep going. Once you see the ticket booth, pay your toll, and on the right-hand side you'll see a large hotel. That's a good place to stay tonight."

"Thank you, officers. Have a good night!"

I approached the hotel, pulled into the parking lot, and looked up. Then I noticed a smaller hotel across the street — not fancy, just a basic budget motel. I turned my wheel toward it, but God said, *"Turn around. You stay here tonight."*

I was cold, tired, and grouchy. "God," I said with a sourpuss face, "I just want to lay my head down. But if you want me to spend more money, then fine!"

In the beautiful Sheraton lobby, standing under the sparkling chandelier, I handed over $150 for the night's stay. The pleasant concierge guided me to my plush room. After a good night's rest under a goose-down comforter, I woke up ready to eat breakfast and get on my way. But when I looked out the window, all the cars were covered in snow — and so were the roads. I called the Navy Chaplain's office to explain my situation. I didn't want them to think I'd gone AWOL. I took myself to breakfast.

As I was eating, I noticed a big, well-dressed, boisterous group that was obviously a church congregation with their pastor. They were all laughing and giggling — much like the group of ladies I had met after my conversion with Father Benedict. It made me smile.

Since I was stuck at the hotel, I went to the gym to work out. A few minutes later, the same fun-loving group entered. They were led by the elegant, heavy-set Black woman who had presided over the breakfast table. As they talked, they kept calling her the "First Lady."

Curious, I approached her and asked, "Ma'am, why are they calling you the First Lady?"

She responded, "Hello, dear. They call me 'First Lady' because my husband is the pastor of our Pentecostal church." Her white tee shirt was adorned with three chunky necklaces, and she wore dressy shorts and flashy pointed-toe flats — a bit out of place for a sweaty gym. "I'm Tenesa," she said, reaching out her ring-covered hand.

"I'm Fenix," I said, shaking it. "I just gave my life to Christ two nights ago."

She asked, "Were you baptized?"

"I need to be baptized?"

The First Lady ignored my question and turned toward her husband. "Pastor," she cooed, and beckoned with her index finger. Her rings flashed under the fluorescent lights. "There's a young lady here you need to meet."

The pastor walked up to me. "Hello — I saw you at the restaurant downstairs."

"Yes, you did. It was nice to watch all of you enjoy your morning together."

The First Lady spoke again. "Pastor Jerome, this young lady gave her life to Christ but was not baptized."

Pastor Jerome smoothed his black tee shirt down over his black sweatpants. "Young lady," he asked, "what is your name?"

"I'm Fenix."

"Fenix, did you give your life to Christ?"

"I was speaking to a Navy Chaplain," I explained. "He asked me to give my life to Christ. I said yes."

Pastor Jerome leaned in. "Were you baptized in water?"

"No — he put his hands on my head and prayed over me."

"We need to baptize you," Pastor Jerome said earnestly. "In water. Right now." He turned toward the door. "Everyone, come with me."

The nine of us — all in our gym gear — followed him down the hall to the hotel Jacuzzi. He walked in fully clothed, shiny black sneakers and all, turned around, and reached out his arm. "Come here, Fenix," he commanded.

I grabbed his hand and stepped into the Jacuzzi. He turned me around, held my nose, and bellowed, "I baptize you in the name of the Father, the Son, and the Holy Spirit. Praise Jesus Christ!" Then he dunked me backward into the hot water.

I was overwhelmed. The group was hollering, clapping, and cheering. It was so sweet, and I felt such a strong sense of community with them.

I was baptized! I had made a conscious decision to get to know Jesus. I felt loved, hopeful, and like something was about to change. God was with me.

Pastor Jerome — dripping head to toe with chlorinated Jacuzzi water — helped me step out onto the tile. "Stay and attend the weekend Christian gathering in the hotel conference room," he said. Everyone agreed, applauding, shouting "Come with us!" and clapping me on the back. Talk about a God moment!

That night, I celebrated with the Christian group through music and prayer. Tears fell down my face. I felt so safe — and I knew God had led me to exactly where He needed me to be. Thankfully, I had heeded His call to stay at the Sheraton!

I kept in touch with Pastor Jerome and First Lady Tenesa. The following week, they invited me to New York to spend the weekend with them at church and in their home. As a small child, I had been forced twice to attend Catholic services, which had always put me to sleep. But this was something I had never experienced before. The pastor was filled with electric energy, racing back and forth across the platform, singing the Gospel, praising God like I had never seen anyone praise before. Toward the end of the service, Pastor Jerome called on the congregation to come forward. As he touched their foreheads, parishioners fell down, fainting at his touch. I had seen nothing like it — but I wanted to experience it.

Then it happened. Pastor Jerome took the mic and said, "I met this young lady at the conference last week. Don't you know the Lord guided her to the hotel where we were staying to make sure she was baptized in water? Fenix, come here. I know you've been wanting to come up. It's your turn."

I walked up and stood in front of him. He looked at me and moved his feet — running in place in those black sneakers, his black robe flapping — as if he was recharging his battery!

He roared, "Are you ready?"

I cried, "I'm ready!"

The pastor roared again, even louder. "Are you ready to receive the goodness of the Lord?"

"I'm ready!"

Pastor Jerome leaned in, placed his hand on my forehead, and my knees buckled. I fell flat on the floor, tears rushing down my face. An overwhelming surge ran through my body. I had never in my life experienced that kind of loving energy. It was majestic.

The next day, I drove home singing my heart out for the love of God.

A Moment for Reflection
When life felt like it had nothing left to offer, did you ever miss the signs quietly pointing you toward a new direction?

Chapter 3
Releasing First Love

I moved back to the base in Norfolk, Virginia, and continued to work at the Chaplain's office. I found a brand-new church near the base, and that is where I met Sansa.

She was adorable. Long brown hair, big blue eyes, a beautiful smile, and freckles all over her face and body. Five feet three inches tall, she was the kind of young Southern woman who wore soft yellow flouncy Sunday dresses. I loved seeing her at church, and we became fast friends. I learned she was a closeted bisexual — born into a strict religious family that believed being gay was an abomination, she had married an older man she was not in love with. Still, she had a big heart and loved him in her own way. She believed this was what Jesus wanted for her.

Some afternoons, Sansa took me out. While driving, she would grab my hand and hold it as if we were the ones in a relationship. My heart was conflicted — she was married, but she was mesmerizing. I loved every moment we spent together. She invited me to her home while her husband David was at work, led me to her bedroom, and asked me to lie down and hold her. We never kissed. But I felt her affection for me deeply.

During the beginning of my relationship with Sansa, the trial of Jonathan began. That trauma turned my attention away from her.

Jonathan's lawyers argued that the rape kit showing forced penetration could not be used because the doctor who had performed the examination had since retired. They also objected to the testimony of another female sailor from the same ship who had reported Jonathan for raping her — she too had been flown off the ship for coming forward, two weeks before I boarded. It seemed the Navy wanted to sweep sexual assault under the rug.

My lesbian JAG attorney — a force to be reckoned with — was handed new orders mid-trial, and my case was given to two fresh-out-of-naval-school cadets who knew nothing about it. Jonathan's attorneys ate me alive. They used my childhood molestation as evidence to suggest I had consented. There was a sailor from my ship on the jury and a police officer from the ship in the courtroom. I will let you figure that one out.

The trial ended with a "Not Guilty" verdict. I watched Jonathan raise his arms in a victory cheer and shake his lawyers' hands. He had raped two women and walked free. Furious and heartbroken, I held my head high as I walked out of that courtroom — and then drove to the beach, bought a six-pack, and drank every last one.

Then I drove home drunk. The blue lights appeared in my rearview mirror. It was not a good day. I was arrested for my first DUI.

I hated my life.

The judge was lenient. I told him my story, and he gave me a warning, a $450 fine, and a suspended license for a year. The Navy offered me orders anywhere I wanted to go. I chose San Diego. Since I couldn't drive, I asked Sansa to go with me. Her husband reluctantly agreed. I promised to pay all expenses, including her return flight home.

Sansa and I packed my SUV and headed to California, holding hands. On the first night in a hotel, we finally expressed everything we had been holding back. For the rest of the four-day trip, we held nothing back. For the first time in my life, I felt what genuine love was like — even though it was complicated, even though it was an affair. When we arrived at my parents' home, we slept in adjoining rooms connected by a bathroom. She crept into my bed in the night. I could feel her tears. I wiped them away and held her until morning.

The next day, I drove her to the airport. She held me tight and made me promise I would visit her. I did.

Two weeks later, I flew back. We spent the night together. In the evening I said, "Sansa, you need to go home. Your husband will be looking for you."

She didn't listen. "I just want to lie here with you a little longer."

I held her for one last night. In the morning I woke her up. "You need to go. Get dressed."

She kissed me on the lips. "I'll see you at church in about an hour."

I arrived at church. Sansa was nowhere. Thirty minutes into the service, she slipped in and sat beside me. We held hands discreetly.

After the service, she took me outside. "David was looking for me all night. He figured out I was with you. I told him I would never see you again." She looked at me with tears in her eyes. "Fenix, I will never forget you — but I have to do right by David, even if he doesn't make me truly happy. This is the life that was chosen for me."

She held me tight. We said our last goodbye.

I flew back to California with a broken heart. Sansa had taught me how to love without the numbing influence of drugs or alcohol. She was the light in my darkness — the only person who had shown me what safe, unfiltered human love felt like. Losing her hurt in a way nothing else had. Heartbroken, I slipped back into the only armor I knew — bitterness, isolation, and anger.

The next chapter of my life began.

It was early 2004. Determined not to let another man ever touch me, I shaved my head and walked onto my new ship with a chip on my shoulder the size of a boulder. I was not there to make friends. On weekends, I would go ashore, rent a cheap motel, and drink until I passed out.

Then one night changed everything.

I went out with Jasmine, my Uncle John's niece. Before we hit the bar, I handed her my car keys. "Don't let me drive tonight." We drank dollar tequila shots, and the next thing I knew I woke up with my face smashed into the windshield of my SUV wrapped around a pole. Drunk and aggressive, I had apparently bullied Jasmine into giving me back my keys, run a red light, hit a car driven by an elderly woman, and crashed into a light pole. Thankfully she was unhurt. I was black and blue all over. The cop yanked me out of the car, slammed me against the hood, and cuffed me. "You could have killed that woman. You're going to jail."

I spent the night behind bars. Because the accident happened off base, I avoided military jail and a dishonorable discharge — God was watching over me even then. My commander sent me for alcohol treatment, and after a month, I returned to my ship and prepared to deploy to Afghanistan.

On that seven-month deployment, God placed someone in my life at exactly the right moment. Chief Petty Officer Frances — a Christian, my superior, and one of the kindest people I have ever known. She prayed with me, showed me grace, and kept me sober. Whenever we were on leave, I didn't drink. I know with everything in me that if Frances had not been on that deployment, things would have gone very differently for me. She was there to protect me — just like the elderly man who once saved me from a predator.

When we came home, I had three months left on my contract. I was done. I walked off that ship and said goodbye only to Frances. I saw a military psychiatrist, pleaded for my release, and was given an honorable discharge.

It was early 2005. Free from the military, I found work as a cook at a fancy hotel — and fell back in with a drug dealer who sold meth. I slipped off the wagon. But this time, something was different. Since my baptism, I began seeing things I had never seen before.

I had purchased a small condo in a low-income neighborhood in San Diego. Mom and Dad came to visit, and Mom bought me an oil painting as a housewarming gift — panels of dark colors, burgundy and navy and brown. I hung it in the living room. A few nights later, from the corner of my eye, I started seeing strange, evil-looking faces in the canvas. I told myself it was drug-induced paranoia. I sobered up for two weeks. The faces remained.

One evening, tired after a long day of cooking, I sat on my couch — and felt something like hands grabbing my thighs. I looked down and saw two handprints on my jeans. I jumped up, moved to the other couch. The same thing happened again. Then something grabbed my ears from behind. They burned. I ran to the bathroom, locked the door, and dropped to my knees.

"God, please protect me. An evil entity is haunting me."

I prayed until I found the courage to open the door. When I did, my apartment was filled with a supernatural light. I fell into a deep, peaceful sleep.

The taunting continued. One evening while sweeping the kitchen, a horrific growl came from the painting — so loud that Poppi, my new cat that I rescued from the pound bolted for the bedroom with every hair on end. I dropped my broom and ran outside, fell to my knees on the grass, and prayed for help. Friends who visited saw nothing in the painting. I began to wonder if I was losing my mind.

Then one evening, a friend named Gabriella invited me out. I got dressed up and walked into a bar, and across the room, I noticed a blonde woman with blue eyes watching me. She walked over, lit a cigarette, threw her head back, and blew out a long trail of smoke. "You look like Liza."

"Who's Liza?" I asked.

She giggled. "Liza Minnelli."

We exchanged numbers. On our first date, I blurted out my entire story. She looked at me and said, "I need to save you."

Well — I needed a savior. And that is where it all began. Her name was Diane.

We dated on and off for six months while I got off meth. If I was going to be in a relationship, I had to stop using drugs. I chose love instead. Diane and I would spend the next fifteen years together.

When she moved into the condo, I asked if she saw anything strange in the painting. She saw nothing — until one night she came into the bedroom shaken. "I see what you see. I see them all. Every single one."

We stood together and watched the figures shapeshift in the canvas. I grabbed a chef's knife from the kitchen, hauled the painting to the dumpster, and slashed it over and over. No one would ever hang that thing on their wall.

I hadn't been crazy. But destroying that painting didn't bring peace. It only revealed the demon I still had to face — the one inside of me.

For the next two years, my drinking reached a new level. Diane drank with me. I would get drunk, she would get angry, we would fight — and when I fought, I became rageful. I smashed things, screamed, blacked out. I had become the chaos I had always run from.

I told her to leave — that I was unlovable, broken. But she stayed. No matter how terribly I treated her, she stayed. Diane ultimately got me through to the other side of addiction. I will always be grateful for that.

By 2008, we had moved into a beautiful three-bedroom townhome in Chula Vista and gotten a new boxer puppy — Marley. Poppi loved Marley immediately. New place, new dog, new life. What could go wrong?

Everything.

With no meth to suppress my emotional wrath, everything I had never healed began to surface. No drugs. No meds. No therapy. No coping skills. No self-love. I was drowning in unprocessed trauma — childhood molestation, military assaults, PTSD, insomnia, psychosis, paranoia. I smashed glasses, drove drunk, screamed until my voice gave out. I was on a quiet quest for death. But death kept running from me.

Things deteriorated until I forced Diane to leave to protect her from me. She took Marley and got an apartment. I drove to my sister Jane's place in Irvine. She greeted me with hugs and tears. "Stay as long as you want. Stay sober and get better."

Three months later, sober and determined, I went back to San Diego. Diane moved back in. Things were okay — until they weren't.

We found a church across the street and I decided to give God another chance. The second Sunday, I introduced myself to the pastor.

"My girlfriend and I just moved in across the street," I said warmly.

He looked at me. "Are you gay?"

"Yes. Do you believe it's a sin?"

He was quiet for a long moment. Then — "Yes. It's a sin to be gay."

I thanked him and walked out. Every time I tried to step through a church door, something tried to shut it in my face. But I was learning — slowly — that finding God does not require a building or someone else's permission.

After that encounter, something dark moved back into our home.

One night at 3:00 a.m., God's voice pulled me out of a dead sleep. *"Wake up. Go get Diane."* I found the guest bedroom locked. No answer to my knocking. I found the spare key, opened the door, and found Diane stretched out on the bed — arms and legs akimbo, frozen, eyes wide with terror. I carried her to our room.

Once she could breathe again, she told me what had happened. "There was a demon pretending to be you. It crawled on top of me and pulled off the blankets. I couldn't move or speak. Then you knocked — and it showed its real face. Pale white. Pitch-black eyes. Scars everywhere."

I grabbed my Bible and opened to Psalm 91. I shouted the verses into the room.

Diane interrupted me. "It's laughing at you."

I put the Bible down and held her until we both fell asleep.

Things spiraled. I started drinking heavily again and engaging in self-harm. I was in spiritual warfare and losing. One morning I blacked out on whisky. Diane came home to a destroyed house. She was on the floor.

"What happened?"

"You attacked me," she wept. "I came home and you were smashing everything. I tried to stop you and you punched me."

The police arrived. I went upstairs, swallowed a bottle of Xanax, and came back downstairs to kneel at the front door and wait for the cuffs.

At the detention center, a female sheriff found me — violently drunk, vomiting on myself. She uncuffed me, let me clean up, and said quietly, "I just got off the phone with your girlfriend. She told me about your life. Don't you think it's time to heal? Don't you think you deserve it — so you can go live your life?"

She opened a cell with a bed, brought me a pillow and a blanket, and let me sleep.

The next morning I went home and cleaned up the devastation. That sheriff had planted a seed of hope.

Something has to change. It has to start with me.

I walked into my office and saw myself in the mirror — one of the few things I hadn't destroyed. I fell to my knees and sobbed.

"God, why am I so sick? Did you make me gay to condemn me? Why am I so lost and broken? Why don't you love me?"

God's Spirit settled over me like a warm hand.

"I made you perfect. I love you."

Those seven words were enough.

I packed a bag and drove myself to the Veterans Hospital. I walked up to the admissions desk and said, "I need to be admitted for addiction. If you don't have a bed, I have a plan — I'll run onto the freeway and get hit by a car. So tell me. Do you have a bed or not?"

"We'll help you," the attendant said. "Please don't leave."

I was an inpatient for the next ninety days — thirty days of detox, sixty days of boot-camp sobriety. While I was inside, Diane helped me short-sell the condo. She rented us an apartment and created a home for me to return to.

It would be dishonest to say I stayed perfectly sober after that. But the uncontrollable rage had left me. The healing had begun.

We eventually moved into a home thirty minutes outside San Diego — all brick and wood paneling, with a big backyard full of orange and lemon trees. Marley and our new boxer puppy Teddy ran wild out there. Poppi climbed the trees and watched over them from above. It was domestic bliss.

Then I had a major car accident.

Diane's cousin Travis was visiting and wanted to test-drive a Camaro at a dealership. The salesperson signed a waiver for a freeway test. Within one minute of merging, traffic stopped dead ahead. A woman texting behind us never noticed. Her SUV struck us at seventy-five miles per hour. The Camaro was totaled.

The result: a traumatic brain injury, four dislocated discs, damaged sciatic nerves, and nerve damage in my right shoulder. Three days in the hospital. Three years of painful therapy. One year walking with a cane.

I believe that accident was God's way of slowing me down — forcing me to stop running and start healing. It was a painful blessing in disguise.

What happened spiritually in the months that followed would cause me to confront my soul in ways I never had before.

God was about to show me how my life would end if I kept drinking it away.

> **A Moment for Reflection**
> Have you loved someone deeply who could never fully love you back, and found yourself learning something sacred in that heartbreak anyway?

Chapter 4
Surrendering to Heal

Mom told me that my dear Uncle John — who, like me, was an alcoholic — had ended up in the hospital, suffering the agonizing pain of cirrhosis of the liver. I drove to see him.

"Hey Uncle John, I came to see you. How you feeling?" I said, happy to see him. He was sitting up in bed.

"Hey, Sport. I am just having a minor issue with my liver." He smiled.

"Are you still drinking?"

"Ah, you know — just my regular martinis every night. I only have two of them. I should be outta here in a couple of days."

"Okay, please get well. And then we can talk about stopping those two martinis until you get better, okay?"

"How have you been?" he asked.

"I'm getting better. I'm working on myself and trying to cut drinking out of my life. Little by little, it's getting better. I'll come visit you in a couple of days and check on you." I kissed him and hugged him goodbye — not knowing he would soon die.

Uncle John and I used to get drunk together. We'd party at his home for hours. His wife didn't like me because I encouraged his drinking.

The next day, my mother called.

"Mija, your uncle just got sedated. His health is declining. We are coming down to San Diego to be with him."

I was confused. "What? I just saw him last night."

"Come meet us at the hospital. We should arrive in about five hours. We will call you when we get there."

When I arrived, I walked to where he was lying in the hospital bed, staring at all the medical equipment hooked up to him. A breathing tube was down his throat. I couldn't believe what was happening. A month later, he died a slow, excruciating death.

The night my uncle died, I went to see his daughter, my cousin Stacey. She gave me a pair of onyx cufflinks with a gold design and one of his favorite Hawaiian shirts — dark blue with palm trees, a beach, and ocean images on it. When I got home, I hung the shirt in my walk-in closet to remember him by and placed the cufflinks in my jewelry box.

The next morning after Uncle John passed, I stayed in bed a little longer than usual. Diane left for work. I got up to use the bathroom, which was next to the closet.

Knock. Knock. Knock.

Three knocks came from inside the closet. I looked in and saw my uncle's shirt hanging on the built-in shoe rack — not where I had hung it. Chills flashed down my spine. I took a photo on my phone. I walked deeper into the closet and said, "Uncle John, are you here?" His Hawaiian shirt moved back and forth, the fabric folding into itself, animating the beach scene like a swelling tide.

I called Diane, who didn't know I had Uncle John's things. "Diane, did you hang Uncle John's shirt at the entrance to my closet?"

"No," she said.

I hung the shirt back with my clothes. The next morning, Diane and I were lying in bed when three knocks came from the closet again. I got up and walked in. Once again, the shirt was hanging in the same place on the shoe rack. "Honey," I said, "the shirt is back on the shoe rack."

Diane said, "Maybe that's your uncle's way of saying you need to stop drinking — or you'll die the way he did."

I said nothing. I grabbed the shirt and hung it back with my clothes.

The next day, a friend came to visit. As I was giving her a tour of the house, I showed her the walk-in closet. Uncle John's cufflinks were sitting on the shoe rack — right in front of a pair of shoes, exactly where the shirt had hung previously. I felt him warning me: *Stop drinking, or you'll have a tormented death like mine.*

"I hear you, Uncle," I said. "I promise I will slow my drinking down." After that night — once I had responded to his signs — his spirit left.

Thank you, Uncle John, for being there for me.

In 2015, Diane and I moved back into the heart of San Diego. I reconnected with Sue — a former drug dealer I had known years earlier. She was now sober, happy, and drug-free. As we stood in the vegetable aisle at Choices market, we apologized to each other for the past. She invited me to her church. It had been eight years since I had been baptized, and I was leery of judgmental religious environments. But here we were — two ex-addicts, healing — so I took a chance.

The church was large and prosperous. The ministers each parked in their private spots in their shiny new Mercedes-Benzes. That day, Pastor Jim took the stage to resounding applause from the packed congregation. His service was polished and welcoming, and I enjoyed it enough to go back.

The second time Sue and I attended, the presenter was a guest — Pastor Malik, one of those ministers who sends a surge of love through you when his hand touches your forehead. I went wearing my Sunday best. While his assistants were escorting parishioners toward the stage, I marched past everyone — even bypassing ushers who tried to stop me — and walked right up. "Touch my forehead, Pastor Malik," I said. He did. I fell to my knees, a wave of love pulsing through me. The congregation clapped. Sue jumped up crying. "I'm so happy for you," she said, hugging me. I sat down and enjoyed the rest of the service.

But the following Sunday, everything changed.

A different pastor spoke — Pastor Jude, a middle-aged, slender, tall man from Arizona. His tone was aggressive and his attitude forceful as he commanded the congregation to hate gay people. "They are not God's children," he thundered from the pulpit. "They are sinners. We must shut them out of our congregation."

I was disgusted and heartbroken. I never went back to that church again.

I kept searching. I met a woman named Nancy at a social event — a masseuse — and hired her for a session at her home. When I was lying on her table, face up and fully relaxed, she leaned over me, her long curly red hair falling into my eyes. Her face contorted into a grimace and she hissed, "Treat me like I'm Jesus right now, Fenix. Tell me your sins. You know it's a sin to be gay. Let it out. Let it all go."

Tears streamed from my eyes. Shame burned through my chest, neck, and face. I needed to get out. "Okay," I said. "Thanks for the massage." I pushed past her, grabbed my clothes, and fled.

But as I walked through the living room toward the door, I was stopped by her friend Clara — sitting on the couch, short, with shoulder-length brown hair and round glasses. She stood up and blocked my way. "Hi, Fenix. Please don't leave. I'd like to talk to you." She sat back down and patted the seat beside her.

Tapping my knee with one hand and twisting a sweater button with the other, she cooed in a sweet but condescending voice, "How do you do it? How do you love Jesus and know you are condemned?"

My heart sank into my stomach. "Thank you," I said. "I have to go." I leapt up and was out the door in a flash.

I wanted nothing to do with Jesus again. I was done.

I only wanted a relationship with God. I didn't yet understand that Jesus was not only God and all about unconditional love — that people had made Him into something He never really was. But over the months that followed, I dedicated myself to opening fully to my conversation with the Divine. In my meditations and quiet moments, I connected with God, and I knew He loved me. He was showing me a love I had never experienced before.

I needed to set ground rules.

"God," I said, "I'm going to set boundaries to protect myself, and here's what they are." Are you wondering how a human being can set ground rules with God? It's easy. You just do it.

"God, I know you love me. You told me I was made perfect. I will never read the Bible. I will never set foot in a church again, and I will never have another Christian tell me being gay is a sin. If they are wrong — and you're telling me I'm made perfect — then show me. Prove to me that being born gay and loving the same gender is not a sin."

I held God to task. I needed Him to do this so that we could have a meaningful, loving relationship built on trust.

He proved it to me. And everything changed.

It was 2016. For six months, every day after Diane left for work, God led me to our private hill. I wasn't working, so I had time to focus on my life and my healing. He would say, *"Come meet me outside in our private place overlooking the hill."* I would sit on the grass and breathe. I could feel His majestic, loving presence around me. He was healing me.

(If you are wondering how I could hear God — it is only telepathic. Am I a psychic? No. A guru? No. A prophet? No. I believe it is a gift. Some people can hear Him and some cannot — and both are completely okay.)

God said, *"I am the Creator. Do you think I make mistakes? If this is the case, then I am imperfect — yet I am All That Is. I am in everything. Look around you, Fenix. What do you see?"*

"I see the dirt, the rocks, the grass, the sky, the clouds, the trees, the leaves," I replied.

"Fenix, I AM all. You touch this tree — I am there. You rub your hands across the grass — I am there. You see the blue sky and clouds — I am there. Everything I create is with love, because Love is all I am."

While I was spending time on the hill with God daily, the Veterans Hospital scheduled me for mental health therapy twice a week. I attended different mental health programs at the VA and learned cognitive-behavioral therapy, dialectical behavioral therapy, and eye movement desensitization and reprocessing. I underwent transcranial magnetic stimulation — a practitioner would place a hood with sensors on my skull and send electronic pulses into my brain to lift the depression. It was remarkable. I learned how to communicate my feelings, change negative thoughts to positive ones, and view situations through a different lens. I was starting to see how I could create my own story — and that God was the throughline.

The Chaplain's Office at the VA was offering weekly meditation classes, and I attended faithfully. Between the meditation and the therapy, I was releasing a lifetime of shame, guilt, and baggage. I became less reactive, more responsive, gentler in all situations and with my words. God was changing me from the inside out.

I was working out and taking Marley and Teddy on nature hikes almost daily. People around me noticed. "You're looking good, Fenix." "You seem happy." "Keep doing what you're doing." And I was happy — genuinely, deeply happy — for the first time.

Every day I went into my spare bedroom, lit a white candle adorned with the Lord's Prayer, put on my headphones with 528 Hz meditation music, and sat in my office chair and meditated for forty minutes. Then I prayed, journaled, and took my dogs for walks. Healing was my full-time job.

And it was working.

I was being rebuilt from the inside out.

And God was just getting started.

> **A Moment for Reflection**
> Is there a mirror in your life — a person whose pain reflects your own — whose story is quietly asking you to finally surrender?

Chapter 5

Letting Go

Even though I was healing — and I truly was — my marriage to Diane was quietly dissolving around me. I was transforming. I wanted a different life: a sober life, better health, a better mindset. I wanted to stay on the path God had taken me on. But Diane and I were growing apart. We weren't connecting anymore. We were more like friends than lovers. We had different friends, and we lived separate lives.

In my heart, I had always known Diane was never really "the one." She had felt she needed to save me from myself — but I no longer needed a savior. I had God. She wasn't interested in healing with me or in healing our marriage. Every time I suggested couples counseling, she refused.

One morning, after Diane came home from the night shift at the hospital, I was sitting in the living room in my grey sweats drinking my first cup of coffee. Diane went into the kitchen to grab a cup. I followed her. "Diane," I said, "I think we should get a divorce."

She turned to me. "A divorce? Are you kidding me? *A divorce?!* You are so selfish, Fenix. I have been there for you all these years, and now you want a divorce?"

"You don't even touch me anymore," I said. "I've been very lonely. I don't think you have forgiven me for my PTSD past. This will give you a chance at finding love — and I can have a chance at a fresh start with someone who won't hold a grudge against me."

She snatched a picture frame from the bookshelf and hurled it at me. It struck my forehead and it hurt like hell. I sat down and cried. I think all the years of meanness I had shown her had finally come right back at me.

I stayed calm. This was my moment to show myself that I had actually learned what my therapist had been teaching me. But Diane lost it completely. She grabbed her phone, got on social media, and asked her friends for divorce attorney recommendations. Then she walked into the bedroom and slammed the door. I left to stay with neighbors and give her space.

The next day, I took her to the courthouse to file. Diane was devastated — but I believed we both deserved the chance to find real love. Four days later, she called me back. She told me something that broke my heart and helped me understand her distance, her coldness, her disconnection. I wanted to stay and help her through it. But her behavior overwhelmed me. After a few weeks, she convinced me to give our marriage another chance. I did — for the sake of the vows we had taken and for the years we had shared. I stopped the divorce.

I went to God. "God, I am so sorry for putting my wife through this. I almost divorced her and dishonored my vow."

God said, *"Do you love her?"*

"Yes, I love her."

"Are you happy?"

"Yes. I saved my marriage."

"Buy her a ring."

I heard God clearly. I bought Diane a new ring — a 1.5-carat gold marquis diamond with a cluster of diamonds encircling it. Even though in my heart I was not in love with her, I loved her. I was loyal. We gave it our best shot. Or at least I did.

What I didn't know was that Diane had been falling in love with one of our closest friends — Amanda, who was married to our dear friend Janis. I didn't know she was having an affair. I was busy trying to build a new life for us, continuing to heal, not just for me but for her.

Our lease was ending in 2017, and I was ready to be a homeowner again. I prayed, and God guided me to a home that had only been on the market for fifteen days. It was in our price range — a three-bedroom American dream home with a white picket fence, a two-car garage, a fully remodeled interior, and a pool with a fence to keep the animals safe. I started a small pet product business called Marley's Planet — dog treats, dog food, and dog beer — and sold them at local farmers' markets. Marley, my emotional support dog, became a little local celebrity. We even made it onto the television news, and Petco's sister stores picked up my products. For several years, the company did well while I kept working on my mental health, staying in therapy, and deepening my relationship with God.

From the outside, our lives looked perfect.

But I felt resentful. Diane and I had gone back to the same pattern — I have my life, you have yours. This wasn't a marriage. It was a business partnership. And I was carrying the full load — cleaning the house, doing the laundry, cooking, grocery shopping, cleaning up after the animals, and running Marley's Planet five days a week at farmers' markets while also preparing all the products in an industrial kitchen.

It was 2019. Things had seriously changed — and not for the better.

God began showing me things I did not want to see.

During prayer, He revealed Diane's affair to me like a movie unfolding in my mind — the timeline, the hotel stays, the lies. My body temperature dropped. I shook uncontrollably.

The next morning, I sat Diane down on the couch. "Are you having an affair with Amanda?"

"No," she said. "We're just friends. She's going through a rough time in her marriage. She needs me."

I wanted to believe her. But the visions had been too clear, too specific. Over the weeks that followed, Diane barely tried to hide what was happening. She stayed out late, spent money recklessly, and grew increasingly distant and aggressive — as if our roles had completely reversed. It was as if her guilt was turning into hostility toward me, the person she was betraying.

I endured it. I believed it was my karma for how I had once treated her. I stayed sober throughout all of it — keeping the promise I had made to God, even when every part of me was in pain.

Finally, Diane invited me out to dinner. I thought she was coming to her senses. But when we left the restaurant and were walking to the car, she stopped and turned to me.

"I feel numb," she said, adjusting the collar of her black silk shirt.

"About us?" I asked.

"Yes. I want a divorce."

I stopped walking. "Why?"

She tossed a few strands of long blonde hair across her shoulder and looked at me. "I want to be a mom, and you don't."

"You're right. I don't. Are you sure?"

"Yes. I'm your best friend and I love you. I just think we've outgrown each other."

That evening, I went to the beach alone. The sun was going down. I was devastated — not just by the divorce, but by what Diane had told me: that God had been coming to her in dreams, telling her to let me go.

"God," I said, standing at the water's edge, "I cannot believe you would tell her to let me go. I know you have a calling on my life, and I will serve you till my last breath. But why? I'm confused. Yet I love you. I promise I will be a better wife. Just please — heal my marriage. No matter what, I surrender to your will."

I fell to my knees with my hands over my face, crying. Because deep inside, I already knew — this divorce needed to happen. I was just terrified of being alone.

Diane had been all I had known for fifteen years. She was the only one who loved me when I was lost, when I couldn't love myself. And now she was ready to love someone else.

When I got home, I went into the guest bathroom, locked the door, turned on the faucet, and got down on my knees. With tears streaming down my face I prayed, "God, I need your help. Save my marriage. Tell me what's going on. Why is this happening? I'm so confused."

God spoke. *"Let her go. I have another for you.* Then He showed me a face but not the whole face. A woman with big brown eyes, fair skin and dark hair.

I opened my eyes in disbelief — and then in peace.

I washed my face, walked to the bedroom, and said clearly, "Diane, it's okay. I'll give you the divorce. God has someone else for me." I crawled into bed beside her. "We have to do this."

The next morning, Diane woke up with tears in her eyes. "I saw Jesus taking you with Him," she said. "He was ready to be your teacher. I saw your mind growing. You were walking next to Him — leaving with Him. It was as if you had become a monk."

For the next month, we tried to be amiable. When it came to splitting our assets, she wanted everything. Every attorney I spoke with told me to fight. But I went within and asked God what to do.

"Fight for nothing. Walk away."

After fifteen years, I left with my service dog Marley and my clothes.

I believe if I had fought, we would have ended up in debt and the battle would have lasted far longer than it needed to. God was freeing me from everything — and all I needed to do was trust Him.

Being married to Diane was a practice run for my real marriage. I learned so much — about myself, about how to treat someone you love, about what I would do differently and what I would never repeat. Diane and I will never speak again, and that chapter of my life is closed. There is no need to look in the rearview mirror.

It was time to heal. It was time to move forward.

After we separated and filed the divorce papers, I made it my mission to go deep with God. I kept up my therapy, stayed sober, hired personal fitness trainers, and committed to rebuilding myself from the ground up. It was 2020. I was divorced and alone.

Then COVID-19 shut everything down.

I was isolated — but this was God's time to have me all to Himself. He would teach me about who I was, about Scripture, about Jesus and His mission. God asked me to sell what I could of Marley's Planet and close the rest. He was releasing me from everything that had been holding me back.

What I didn't realize then was that God was preparing me for a completely different life. A life full of adventure, abundance, new friends, new opportunities, deeper consciousness, more love, a new body, and a renewed heart and mind.

I was about to be reborn.

A Moment for Reflection
What in your life is God asking you to release right now — and what might be waiting for you on the other side of that surrender?

Then there was Grace . . .

Chapter 6
Seeing Signs from Beyond

"Each person goes into the light according to his own choosing.
Those who choose it will receive it."
—Gospel of Philip

From this point on, I am sharing conversations I had with God. These are lessons I learned, though not always in chronological order. What I know is this: God is loving, kind, patient, gentle, and humble. He is a giver, a protector, a mentor, my friend, and at times when needed, a father who corrects me. He is the breath in my lungs.

It was 2017, before God blessed me with the Holy Spirit.

"God," I asked, "why is there so much hate in this world?"

God replied, *"Because humanity has free will to choose love or hate. Human beings have total control over their emotions, feelings, thoughts, and actions. I will not intercede. However, those who choose to express evil experience karma."*

When God spoke those words, I understood something I had been circling for years. He did not create puppets He could control. He created beings capable of unconditional love — with the power within them to create their own reality. But love cannot exist without freedom, and freedom means we can choose fear, pride, greed, or violence. Our capacity to choose is where good and evil begin. Evil is not sent by God — it is what happens when human beings who have forgotten love misuse their freedom. If God removed that choice, love would no longer be love. It would be programming.

I wanted to choose good. I saw how the evil in my own life had paved a road that eventually led me toward the light. The stories that follow are how I learned my lessons — and how that knowledge transformed my life.

The $24,000 Lesson

When I was twenty-one, I was a meth addict — angry, boundaryless, and capable of things I am not proud of. When my then-girlfriend Alyssa was leaving me, I went to the bank and transferred her balance — $24,000 — into my personal account. I cleaned her out. That evening she realized what I had done. She was furious. She had every right to be.

I knew what I had done was wrong. I knew it the moment I did it. And I knew that one day I would face the karma for it.

Twenty years later, the reckoning came.

I was forty-two, going through my divorce from Diane, and working to expand my pet product business. At a conference, I saw a speaker onstage who seemed credible and knowledgeable. Her price for services was $24,000. I hired her. She took my money and ran. Later I met others she had defrauded. She was a fraud and a thief — exactly what I had been to Alyssa.

That was my karma.

I have tried to apologize to Alyssa three times, intending to offer to pay her back. She never wants to speak to me. Whether or not she has forgiven me I will never know. What I do know is that God forgives — and I have forgiven myself. As Matthew 6:14–15 (KJV) tells us, forgiveness is the pathway to freedom — for both the one who was wronged and the one who did the wronging.

Questions on the Hill

One sunny San Diego day I sat on our hill with God, and I asked Him the questions that had been living in me for years.

"Did the Bible come from you?"

"No," God said. "It was inspired by Me and written through the thoughts of man — who, like you, wanted to give voice to their visions, voices, and feelings regarding who I AM."

"Is Jesus the Son of God?"

"Yes. And you are my child as well."

I shielded my eyes from the sun and looked up. "But are you Jesus?"

"I AM He who sent Jesus."

"Then who are you?"

"I AM the Creator of all — the Alpha and the Omega, the beginning and the end. I am in everything, in all places. I am the Divine, the Light of this world. I AM that I AM."

I was falling in love for the very first time — not with a person, but with God. And it was the love I had always been searching for. My life was changing. I was waking up calm, rested, peaceful, and joyful. Not just happy — joyful. And those are not the same thing.

Happiness is a pleasant emotional state — external, fleeting, dependent on circumstances. Joy is something deeper. It is a stable, internal sense of well-being that does not require the world to cooperate. The more time I spent in God's presence, asking questions and listening for answers, the more joy became my default. Not because my life was perfect — but because I was finally aligned with the source of life itself.

Reclaiming Scripture

There was still one question burning at the center of everything: *How could I be happy when I had been told my whole life that I was a sicko lesbian?* My father's words were still burned into my soul. So I brought that question to God too.

He guided me to research. And what I found there set me free.

Before the mid-twentieth century, no Bible — Hebrew, Greek, Latin, or English — used the modern word *homosexual.* That term entered English Bibles only in 1946. Earlier translations described specific exploitative or ritualistic behavior — not loving, consensual relationships. Even the 1611 King James Version never uses the word. When Jesus summarized the entire law, He said simply: *"Thou shalt love the Lord thy God with all thy heart… and thy neighbor as thyself"* (Matthew 22:37–39, KJV). He made no list of exclusions. Love was the highest commandment — the measure of all righteousness.

The passage most often used against people like me — 1 Corinthians 6:9–11 — is almost always quoted incompletely. People stop before verse 11, which says: *"And such were some of you: but ye are washed, but ye are sanctified, but ye are justified in the name of the Lord Jesus."* That verse is God's declaration that we are washed clean.

The ancient Greek words used in that passage — *malakoi* and *arsenokoitai* — described luxury, passivity, and sexual exploitation, not orientation or mutual love. When later translators rendered those words as "homosexuals," they applied a modern concept to an ancient world that had no such category.

Jesus never said a single word about same-sex relationships. But He spent His entire ministry loving the people religion had rejected — touching lepers, dining with sinners, defending women, blessing foreigners. He was not policing who we love. He was healing how we love.

What Sodom Was Actually About

For years I was told God destroyed Sodom because men loved men. When I read the text myself — in the original Hebrew, in the King James Bible — I found something completely different.

In Genesis 19, the men of Sodom surrounded Lot's house and demanded his guests be brought out so they could *"know them"* — a word used in Scripture for violent sexual violation, not loving relationship. This was threatened gang rape — an act of domination, power, and cruelty. Not love. Not attraction. Brutality.

And when the prophets explained Sodom's sin directly, none of them mentioned sexuality. Ezekiel 16:49–50 (KJV) says: *"Behold, this was the iniquity of thy sister Sodom — pride, fullness of bread, and abundance of idleness… neither did she strengthen the hand of the poor and needy."* Pride. Greed. Neglect of the vulnerable. That was Sodom's sin.

When Jesus Himself referenced Sodom — in Matthew 10:14–15 and Luke 10:10–12 — He connected its guilt to inhospitality, not sexuality. In ancient Near Eastern culture, hospitality to strangers was sacred. To assault them was to commit the ultimate evil.

Sodom was not condemned for love. It was condemned for cruelty.

I hope you understand, dear reader, that this truth is not theoretical for me. It is lived, prayed through, and rooted in my own experience of God's love. Being gay does not separate anyone from God. Fear and shame do. When love is genuine, kind, and respectful — it mirrors the divine.

Christ spent His ministry loving those religion had cast out. I am one of them. And so, perhaps, are you.

Let what God showed me set you free.

> **A Moment for Reflection**
> If you truly believed that God gave you free will out of love, how would you begin to take ownership of the choices that brought pain into your life.

Chapter 7
Missing the Mark

"This ignorance of the Father brought about terror and fear.
And terror became dense like a fog, so no one was able to see.
Because of this, error became strong."
—The Gospel of Truth

Earlier I said that when God called me, I came running. I'd leave my home and go to our private place overlooking the hill. "God," I said one day, "after doing my best research and you showing me you love me, again I am asking you, is being gay a sin? And since I am married to Diane, am I living in sin? And what is sin?"

God said, "No, you are not sinning for being married to Diane and for loving her. How could I ever condemn that which I AM. I am Love, and when you are loving each other, we are One. You were not born to be defined by sin, but let's understand the word *sin* as error, to go astray, or missed mark."

I walked back and forth across the grass and stretched my legs. I'm sure anyone who saw me waving my arms and talking to the air would have thought I was a crazy person. "What do you mean we're not born in sin? The Bible says we're born in sin."

God said, "You are born into a broken world with sinful conditions. Sin itself is learned, chosen, and practiced."

"Does everyone make mistakes? Yes."

"Fenix-cita," God said, "Remember. There is free will, but when human beings choose to add in their own interpretation, particularly around homosexuality, they miss the mark, and that's what happened, which has caused so much pain for my children."

I stood still for a moment after He said that. *My children.* Not *those people.* Not *sinners.* His children. I had carried the word *sin* like a stone around my neck my entire life — dragged it through every church pew, every moment of self-hatred, every time I had tried to pray myself into being someone different. And now God was telling me the stone was never mine to carry. I needed to understand this more deeply, not just for myself, but for you. So I went and I researched. And what God told me on that hill matched exactly what I found.

I want to be honest with you before I share what God showed me through Scripture. Many faithful, sincere Christians interpret these same passages differently. They see them as upholding the design of male-female union as God's timeless intention for marriage. I honor their love for God and their love for Scripture. After years of prayer, tears, study, and direct encounter with God's affirming love, my heart and conscience found freedom in a different understanding — that the Bible's deepest heart is unconditional love, and that committed, faithful same-sex relationships can reflect that same divine love. I share this not to win a debate, but to offer freedom to anyone still carrying shame they were never meant to carry."

What Is Sin?

In the original Hebrew of the Old Testament, the word *sin*, חָטָא (*chata*), means literally "to miss the mark, or go astray." It is an archery term. If you aimed for the target and your arrow missed, you had *chata'ed*. It wasn't about being evil; it was about failing to hit your intended mark, straying from what is good, true, or aligned with love. So, in Hebrew thought:

1. Sin wasn't permanent.
2. Sin wasn't an identity. We're not meant to be defined by sin.
3. Sin was a *mistake* — a chance to adjust, realign, and try again.

In the New Testament, the Greek word for sin, *ἁμαρτία* (hamartia), also means "to miss the mark." It's the same root metaphor — an archer aiming, but falling short. So when Paul says, "For all have sinned and fall short of the glory of God" (Romans 3:23, KJV), he's not calling humanity inherently wicked. He's acknowledging that everyone misses alignment with divine love sometimes. We lose aim. We forget. We act out of fear or ego instead of compassion.

But the focus of Christ's message wasn't punishment; it was *restoration*. He came to recalibrate the aim, to show what love looks like when it hits the mark.

That's why *repentance* (תְּשׁוּבָה - *teshuvah*) in Hebrew literally means "to return" — to come back home to truth, to balance, to love. Repentance is not groveling. Repentance is *remembering*.

I want to be clear here. In order for us to come back into alignment and to aim better in our actions, behaviors, and thoughts, we need to come to repentance. Why? Because in order for God's laws to stop affecting our lives and to be one with God, we must repent — and I mean always — for all our actions, deeds, behaviors, and thoughts. This is essential if we want a life with God. And it is essential if we want to heal and live with inner peace.

Even in the Twelve Steps, you are asked to make a moral inventory of the exact nature of your wrongs and to admit to God, to yourself, and to another person what you have been doing wrong. This is the way to freedom — a freedom like you have never experienced before. I will make sure to add prayers toward the end of this book to help guide you there.

Jesus's Teaching on Sin: Healing, Not Condemning

I had grown up hearing about a Jesus who pointed fingers, who kept a ledger of wrongs, who turned His back on the broken. But the more I sat with Scripture — really sat with it, not the version handed to me by religion, but the living Word — the more I found someone unrecognizable from what I had been taught. Look at how Jesus actually treated people called "sinners":

1. The adulterous woman: *"Neither do I condemn thee: go, and sin no more."* (John 8:11, KJV)
2. Zacchaeus, the tax collector: Jesus dined with him, and the encounter led Zacchaeus to willingly change his entire life. (Luke 19:1–10, KJV)
3. The prodigal son: The father did not wait for an explanation. He *ran* to embrace his lost child the moment he saw him coming. (Luke 15:11–32, KJV)

Every single story shows sin as a wound to be healed, not a crime to be punished. Jesus never once looked at a broken person and said, *you are too far gone.* He said, *get up, you are loved, now go and aim better.*

How Religion Later Changed the Tone

Over centuries, religious systems — especially through Latin translations — began equating "sin" with moral guilt and legal offense, a crime against God that required punishment or sacrifice. The Latin *peccatum* shifted the word from "missing the mark" to a moral stain — something dirty, shameful, permanent. That is where much of the trauma around "sin" comes from. People were taught they were *born sinful* rather than *born sacred.*

I realized God never condemned who I was. I had to adjust my aim — not to please religion, but to align with love.

I hope you know that God is not defined by sin. All God desires for you is to live more joyfully and freely in love. Let's continue to heal all religious trauma together. Let's hit our mark.

As I shared earlier, I was on drugs; I was an alcoholic. I screamed, threw things across rooms, and got angry quickly. I felt rage. Do you believe I was "missing the mark?" Or "being evil?" I was missing the mark, and I was not well mentally. I was in pain. I needed love, support, and mental health help from doctors and psychologists. I needed to get sober. I used drugs to suppress traumatic memories that were encoded in my subconscious mind.

When I got behind the wheel under the influence of alcohol and played Russian roulette with my life and the lives of others, was I missing the mark? Was I committing an evil act? I am answering this honestly: I was acting in ways that caused real harm. Careless. Thoughtless. Aggressive. I had to pay the price. In my second DUI in 2004, I could have killed that old woman. I would have spent ten years to life in prison for involuntary manslaughter. I deserved my three years of probation, the $10,000 fine, the two years with a breathalyzer, and one year with no license. I paid the price gladly. Was God looking out for that woman and for me? Yes, He was.

It was only after I understood the difference between *missing the mark* and genuine *evil* that I could stop torturing myself for every mistake I had ever made. Because they are not the same thing — not in life, and not in Scripture.

The Difference Between Sin and Evil

Sin means missing the mark, falling short of love. It comes from human imperfection, misunderstanding, or pain. Sin can be corrected, healed, and forgiven. Evil, on the other hand, means harm, corruption, or the intent to destroy. Evil involves a conscious opposition to good. It chooses harm rather than falling short of love. Evil is born of will — it is a deliberate turning away from truth and compassion.

The Hebrew Concept — Ra' (רע)

In Hebrew, the word for evil is *ra'*, which means bad, harmful, or destructive. It isn't always about moral wickedness; sometimes it simply describes something that causes pain or loss. In Genesis, the Tree of the Knowledge of Good and Evil introduces humanity to *tov* (good) and *ra'* (harm) — an awareness of what can destroy, distort, or cause suffering. The prophets also spoke of evil as inversion, when truth and goodness are twisted. Isaiah 5:20 (KJV) says: *"Woe unto them that call evil good, and good evil; that put darkness for light, and light for darkness; that put bitter for sweet, and sweet for bitter."*

Evil in this sense is confusion that replaces love with fear, justice with greed, and compassion with cruelty. In the Hebrew understanding, evil is not simply doing wrong — it is *knowing* what is right and deliberately choosing what causes harm.

In the New Testament, the Greek word for evil is πονηρός (*ponēros*), which means corrupt, harmful, or malicious. It describes something that actively works against life, truth, or love. Jesus often used this word to describe the energy or mindset that resists goodness — a conscious choice to act from fear, greed, hatred, or separation. While sin can be corrected through awareness, evil can only be transformed through light, humility, and divine love.

Evil is the choice to remain in error and to spread it. While sin *forgets* love, evil *rejects* it.

When I saw this difference, I stopped judging myself so harshly. My mistakes were not proof that I was bad; they were reminders that I was still learning. I saw that evil only has power when love is absent. The moment love enters the scene, evil loses its voice. Every shadow disappears in the instant that truth appears. That is the power of love.

At the beginning of this book, I shared the story about the man who was chasing me, trying to capture me. I believe he had intentions of harming or killing me. That was evil. I also recounted my experience with demonic spirits. Were they real? To me, they were. Evil isn't just in the flesh; it comes in spiritual form. I was on drugs; I hated life; I was living in darkness. My mindset was misaligned — and yet, looking back, it was almost as if those dark forces caused me to run straight to God. Could they have recruited me to the dark side? No. They knew that even though I was in agony, all I wanted was to experience love — something they could never give. And so they taunted me and frightened me, and had control over me when I was under the influence.

The last time I saw demonic spirits was in 2010. After I healed and allowed God's love to enter my heart, they never haunted me again. In my experience, heavy drug use and deep emotional pain left me feeling spiritually exposed and vulnerable. My hope is that you will run away from drugs, heal your heart, heal your mind, and turn to love, to light, to God.

And if you are not gay — if you are reading this as a straight person who has simply felt unloved, condemned, or cast out by religion for any reason at all — this chapter is for you too. Shame does not discriminate. It lands on the divorced person who was told God hated their broken marriage. It lands on the addict who was told they were too far gone to be saved. It lands on the abuse survivor who was told to stay silent and forgive without healing. It lands on the veteran who came home broken and found no room for their pain inside a church pew. Shame finds all of us. And so does God's love. Whatever brought you here — you belong in these pages.

Peter once asked Jesus: *"Lord, how often shall my brother sin against me, and I forgive him? Till seven times?"*

Jesus saith unto him, "I say not unto thee, Until seven times: but, Until seventy times seven." (Matthew 18:21–22, KJV)

Seventy times seven. Think about that. That is not a number — that is a *direction*. Keep forgiving. Keep returning. Keep coming home to love.

Forgiveness is the way, the truth, and the life. If you have hurt others, ask for their forgiveness — and then forgive yourself. If you have done things you wish you had never done, forgive yourself. Heal. Turn to God, not religion.

Repentance is necessary — yes. And so is forgiveness, in every layer of your life. Want to feel free from mental illness? Forgive everyone. Want a life where disease loosens its grip? Forgive everyone, including yourself. Want a life filled with inner peace and joy that no one can take away? I am going to say it one last time: forgive everyone, including yourself.

Who is God for you? Maybe your God doesn't have a capital G, and you call it your Higher Power. Is your God the Universe, energy, the Divine Light? God is all those things. God is a divine frequency, and so much more. It is my greatest hope that you will choose to align with the frequency of Love. But above all, it is my greatest hope that you turn to Christ.

The reason I say this is because among all the great spiritual texts — the Bhagavad Gita, the Quran, the teachings of Hinduism and Taoism — only Jesus says, *"I am the Way, the Truth, and the Life. No one comes to the Father except through me."* Only Jesus says that through Him you will have eternal life. And He is the only one returning.

The mark is love. And you were made to hit it.

A Moment for Reflection
What if the shame you have carried about who you are was never God's truth about you, but a human misreading of it?

Chapter 8
Hearing the Voice

"He that loveth not knoweth not God; for God is love."
—1 John 4:8 (KJV)

Love is all. True love has no boundaries — it loves all, always. Love even trumps the commandments of the Old Testament. Love isn't just the love of a family, or the love of a friend, or the love of two people building a life together. Love is the very substance of which the universe is made. In this chapter, we will look at romantic love through the lens of Scripture. Does the Bible advocate love only between a man and a woman — or is there room for other kinds of love? I say there is.

I was married to Diane, but was she the love of my life? No. But I loved her. Did I know, for most of our fifteen years together, that she wasn't "the one?" In my heart, I knew. But I was loyal and faithful. I stayed. She was meant to be in my life for a season, and for the first three years she stuck around even though I was on drugs, an alcoholic, and mentally unstable. She wanted to love me, and I let her. I wanted to heal and love her back. Once I got help, our relationship grew healthier — but we were never a genuine match.

Still, God blessed us. Diane was a blessing. She taught me about love the best way she could. I learned what to do — and what not to do — in a relationship. I learned how to communicate without screaming and slamming doors, how to see things from another person's point of view, and how to compromise. Life is complicated, and the day-to-day weight of it can test our love in ways we never expect. We need to keep flirting with our partners. Keep them laughing. Keep them feeling seen and special.

We didn't do that. And eventually, the distance between us became too wide to cross.

I will always be grateful for that relationship. My time with Diane prepared me to one day meet "the one." It taught me that patience, love, and grace triumph over adversity. As 1 John 4:7 (KJV) says: *"Beloved, let us love one another: for love is of God; and every one that loveth is born of God, and knoweth God."*

God forms every person with His divine love. Each human being is part of His design, connected to the whole and held in balance. From the moment of our conception, we are in conscious relationship with God. We are united in oneness.

So when I began to ask whether my love — the love I felt for women, the love I had given to Diane for fifteen years — was somehow outside of God's design, I had to go back to the very beginning. I had to go back to Genesis. And what I found there changed everything.

The Creation Story: A Poetic Blueprint, Not a Rulebook

Genesis 1 and 2 are not a science lesson or a biological decree. They are a sacred poem, written in the rhythm of Hebrew thought, to describe the balance and unity of all life. When we read Genesis through the lens of symbolism, language, and love, we discover that it was never written to define rigid gender roles or to limit who can love whom. It was written to describe union, balance, and oneness.

"So God created man in his own image, in the image of God created he him; male and female created he them." (Genesis 1:27, KJV)

The Hebrew word for "man" here is אָדָם (*adam*), which does not mean *a male person.* It means *humanity* — literally "earth-being," from *adamah*, meaning earth or clay. God did not create a male gender and a female gender and assign them fixed roles and rules. He created humanity in His divine image, encompassing the union of opposites: masculine and feminine energy. This is oneness expressed as duality — not hierarchy, not separation, not a blueprint for who you are allowed to love.

In Genesis 2:21–23, God causes Adam to sleep and takes a "rib" to make woman. But the Hebrew word for "rib" — צֵלָע (*tsela*) — also means "side" or "half." That changes everything. It is not God performing surgery. It is a poetic image of humanity being divided into two — two energies, two reflections of the same soul. God did not create a lesser companion. He revealed the other side of the divine within us. When Adam says, *"This is now bone of my bones, and flesh of my flesh"* (Genesis 2:23, KJV), he is not naming dominance. He is recognizing *mirroring.*

The "male" and "female" in Genesis represent polarities of being, not physical gender requirements. Masculine energy: active, outward, directive. Feminine energy: receptive, inward, nurturing. Both exist in every person, regardless of gender. God's image is complete only when both energies are held in balance. That is the wholeness God was describing — not a rule about who stands beside whom at an altar.

When religion reduced that sacred metaphor to "a man must marry a woman," it missed the point entirely. God was not defining a sexual order. He was describing spiritual balance.

What "One Flesh" Really Means

"Therefore shall a man leave his father and his mother, and shall cleave unto his wife: and they shall be one flesh." (Genesis 2:24, KJV)

That phrase "one flesh" is not about reproductive anatomy. It is a symbol for what happens when two souls join in authentic love, mutual respect, and devotion. That is the true divine design: union through love, not union through gender.

And if *"He that loveth not knoweth not God; for God is love"* (1 John 4:8, KJV), then any love that mirrors kindness, honesty, and life-giving care reflects the image of God.

Marriage in the Hebrew Bible was never one fixed divine formula. It evolved across centuries, reflecting human culture while God kept calling all people — regardless of circumstance — back to love, fidelity, and sacred union. Abraham, Jacob, David, Solomon — men revered as righteous in Scripture — all had multiple wives and concubines. The form of marriage was cultural, not divinely prescribed.

What God consistently called people toward was not a particular structure. It was *covenant* — the Hebrew word בְּרִית (*berit*): agreement, alliance, sacred promise.

By the time of Jesus, marriage laws were largely patriarchal. Men could divorce for almost any reason. When challenged on this, Jesus pointed not to legal contracts but to the original intention of unity: *"What therefore God hath joined together, let not man put asunder"* (Matthew 19:6, KJV). That was not a gender statement. It was a spiritual principle: when two people are truly joined in divine love, they do not let ego, law, or pride tear apart what God has unified.

And then Jesus said something that has been largely ignored.

What Jesus Said About Those Who Don't Fit the Mold

Immediately after speaking about marriage, Jesus acknowledged something remarkable. He said: *"For there are some eunuchs, which were so born from their mother's womb: and there are some eunuchs, which were made eunuchs of men: and there be eunuchs, which have made themselves eunuchs for the kingdom of heaven's sake. He that is able to receive it, let him receive it."* (Matthew 19:12, KJV)

"Eunuch" in the ancient world was a broad social category — not merely a medical one. It included people who did not marry, did not reproduce, and did not fit the sexual norms of their culture. People who were perceived as "other." Jesus explicitly acknowledged that some people are born outside traditional expectations around marriage and sexuality — and He did so without condemnation, without correction, and without exclusion. He simply said: *he that is able to receive it, let him receive it.*

Jesus saw people like me. And He did not turn away.

What Paul Actually Said — and What He Meant

I know the passage that has been used to wound people like me. I have heard it quoted from pulpits and thrown like a weapon. Romans 1:26–27 (KJV): *"For this cause God gave them up unto vile affections: for even their women did change the natural use into that which is against nature: And likewise also the men, leaving the natural use of the woman, burned in their lust one toward another."*

For years, that passage made me feel like an abomination. But when I finally sat with it — really sat with it, in context, in the original Greek — I found something completely different from what I had been taught.

The key phrase is "against nature" — in Greek, παρὰ φύσιν (*para physin*). It does not mean "against God's design for all people." It means *against one's own nature*. Paul is describing people who acted contrary to their own God-given orientation — people who, driven by lust and idolatry, abandoned who they were created to be.

That is the opposite of my story.

I did not leave a heterosexual desire — I was never given one. I cannot abandon something I never had. I was born gay. It is not a choice. It is not an exchange. It is simply who I am, exactly as God formed me.

The passage says they "burned in their lust." I do not burn in lust. What I have felt — what I have always longed for — is love. Covenant. A sacred partnership built on truth and devotion. The harm Paul was naming was self-betrayal: people using their bodies against their own truth, against their own nature. If I were to force myself into a relationship with a man, *that* would be self-betrayal. *That* would be acting against my nature. *That* would be the very sin Paul was describing.

Paul was calling people to integrity — to live in alignment with who God made them to be, through sacrificial love, not performance. And if two people live in love, mutual respect, and truth, they embody exactly the kind of union that reflects God's heart.

Biblical marriage was never about who stands at the altar. It was about the love at the altar.

What This Means for You

If you are gay, lesbian, or bisexual, I want you to hear this clearly: you are loved by God. Your love is not outside of His design. You are not a mistake. You are not an abomination. You are a soul made in the image of the Divine, and any love you build on honesty, commitment, and care is a love God recognizes.

If you are straight and reading this, I want you to hear this too: the God you serve is bigger than the boundaries religion has drawn around Him. He is not afraid of love. He is love. And He has always been calling all of His children — every single one — back to that.

Jesus summarized everything with two commandments: *"Love God . . . and love your neighbor as yourself. On these two commandments hang all the law."* (Matthew 22:37–40, KJV)

If love is the foundation, then any marriage built on love, honesty, and genuine care fulfills the law — regardless of gender, regardless of tradition.

When I finally understood this, I stopped seeing rules in Scripture and started seeing revelations.

Storytime: Real News

As of this writing, thirty-eight countries around the world now recognize marriage between two loving people, regardless of gender. In Mexico City, where my mother was born, marriages are celebrated between two souls — not defined by "a man and a woman." In the United States, where I was born and where I served my country, the Supreme Court affirmed the dignity of same-sex marriage.

There have been moments of fear along the way. One such moment involved Kim Davis, a former county clerk in Kentucky, who refused to issue a marriage license to a same-sex couple. The couple sued, the courts ruled against her, and her appeal was ultimately declined by the Supreme Court.

During that season of uncertainty, I brought my fears to God. I wondered what the future held — not only for myself, but for so many people who longed for the same dignity others took for granted. In prayer, I heard words that brought me peace: *"It will not be overturned. It will be dismissed."* I didn't fully understand what that meant at the time. But it quieted my fear.

After I moved to Houston, I met many people anxious about the future of marriage equality. I shared with them the peace I had found in prayer — not as a political promise, but as a reminder that God's love for all of us was never in question.

For me, this experience confirmed something I had carried quietly for a long time: being born gay is not a mistake. It is not a flaw. I am made in the image of God, and my heart reflects His love and mercy. Love — honest, committed, life-giving love — has always been at the center of God's story.

And it always will be.

A Moment for Reflection
Have you stayed in a relationship out of loyalty and love, even knowing in your heart it wasn't meant to last forever — and what did that season teach you?

Chapter 9

Honoring Love

"Then said Jesus, Father, forgive them;
for they know not what they do."
—Luke 23:34 (KJV)

When a person says, "The Bible clearly condemns homosexuality," I have learned that argument rarely opens a heart. What opens hearts is love. So I respond with compassion, share what God showed me through prayer and study, and trust Him with the rest.

Jesus Himself modeled how Scripture is meant to be understood — not as frozen law, but as living truth revealed through love. He did not reject Scripture. He fulfilled it by restoring its heart. He showed that God's law was never meant to be wielded as a weapon. It was meant to be lived as love.

What Traditionalists Will Tell You

Many sincere, faithful Christians anchor their understanding in passages they believe speak clearly to this topic. I honor their love for Scripture and their sincerity. Here is what I found when I studied those same passages through the lens of history, language, and the heart of Jesus."

They will quote Leviticus, Romans, Corinthians, and Timothy. They will say the Bible is clear. They will believe it with their whole hearts.

Here is what I want you to know: those passages addressed specific acts — exploitation, idol worship, sexual abuse, and domination. The original Hebrew and Greek words used in those texts do not mean 'homosexual.' The word mishkav zakar in Leviticus referred to specific ritualistic acts tied to pagan worship. The Greek word malakoi in Corinthians meant moral weakness or the abuse of power — not a loving, committed relationship between two people.

What the original Hebrew and Greek reveal is that these passages addressed specific acts of exploitation, idolatry, and abuse — not the kind of faithful, committed, loving relationship I longed for. That distinction set me free.

And if someone asks, "But doesn't the Bible show only male-female love stories?" — yes, those stories were written through the lens of ancient patriarchy, where male-female unions were the expected cultural norm. But even within that framework, Scripture is filled with deep covenantal bonds that echo the heart of God. Ruth said to Naomi: "*. . . for whither thou goest, I will go; and where thou lodgest, I will lodge: thy people shall be my people, and thy God my God.*" (Ruth 1:16–17, KJV)

That is not merely friendship. That is covenant. That is the language of the soul choosing another soul — and God honored it.

The Spirit of God's love appears in all kinds of unions. Scripture honors love that is loyal, kind, and self-giving — not merely heterosexual. I share all of this not as a definitive theological argument, but as the fruit of my own prayerful journey — offered with love to anyone who has been told by religion that God does not love them exactly as they are.

What Jesus Actually Did

I want to show you something. Look at the difference between what the law demanded and what Jesus chose: The law said to separate the clean from the unclean. Jesus touched the leper and healed him. The law said to stone the sinner. Jesus forgave her and restored her. The law said to judge by appearance. Jesus looked straight past it to the heart. The law said keep the rules. Jesus said fulfill them — through love.

When Scripture is used to shame and exclude rather than heal and restore, it is being used in a way that is the opposite of what Christ modeled. Jesus broke the law of separation to fulfill the law of love. That is the Jesus I encountered. That is the Jesus who found me."

He broke the law of separation to fulfill the law of love. He said, *"You have heard it said . . . but I say unto you"* (Matthew 5:21–22, KJV). If love deepens understanding, then interpreting Scripture through love is not rebellion. It is obedience to Christ.

Jesus often spoke in a way that invited reflection rather than debate. He said, *"He that hath ears to hear, let him hear"* (Matthew 11:15, KJV). Truth reveals itself not through argument, but through openness. Scripture unfolds most clearly for those willing to see it with the heart.

Your Strength Comes from Calm Truth

When someone challenges you from a place of fear or rigid doctrine, respond from a place of compassion. You might say: "I understand why you were taught that." I carried those same beliefs for years. But when I brought my deepest questions to God in prayer, and when I studied the language, the history, and the heart of Jesus, I found something far more beautiful than condemnation. I found unconditional love.' You do not need to win the conversation. You only need to love the person in front of you.

Forgive them, as Jesus said from the cross — *"for they know not what they do"* (Luke 23:34, KJV). Love them where they are. Jesus loved the people who were nailing Him to the cross. That is the standard. That is the call.

Love Your Neighbor, Love Your Life

God makes no mistakes. He made you exactly the way you are. So love your neighbor, love your life, and love whomever you are made to love — just do it with honoring, life-giving intentions.

Jesus gave us a simple measure for discerning truth: *"By their fruits ye shall know them"* (Matthew 7:16, KJV).

Shame, fear, self-hatred, and despair are not the fruits of God. Love, healing, integrity, and restored lives are. When Scripture is interpreted in a way that leads people back to love — toward God, toward themselves, and toward one another — it bears the fruit Christ promised.

Abba

When God wanted to connect with me, I no longer needed Him to prove anything about the Bible. I didn't need to ask questions about Scripture. I just desired a loving, open relationship with God. I wanted a father, a mentor, a friend, a healer, and a protector all in one. God is that for me — always, in every moment of my life.

I call Him "Abba," which means "Father." One day I said to Him, "Abba, I know you are both male and female energy, but for me, I need a father — because my dad was absent for most of my life. So if it's okay with you, I'm going to call you Abba instead of God."

God said, "I'm going to call you Fenix-cita."

And just like that, we had our own language. Our own names for each other. That is the kind of God He is.

I understand that when I rely on God's guidance, everything goes well in my life. So I seek Him for everything — my finances, my health, my relationships, my career, my love life, which direction to go. I mean everything. And I asked Him once, "Abba, how is it that I have access to you all day, every day, at any moment?"

He said, "My Fenix-cita, the reason you have access to me at a moment's notice is because you know you can, and you choose to. Anyone can have access to me. You, my beloved, seek me out all the time. Your faith is the size of a mountain — when at one time in your life, it was the size of a mustard seed. It is my desire to have a loving relationship with all my children. And you do. Therefore, I am all yours, always, at all times."

Abba talks with me when I seek Him. And I believe — with everything in me — that if you open your heart in faith, God will meet you there too.

Storytime: Mustard Seed to Mountain

In 2010, I was beginning to heal after my arrest. I wanted to show Diane that I loved her. I bought her a ring — but I gave it to her while I was drunk and we were fighting. I threw it down the hallway. Talk about unromantic. She never wanted to wear it.

By 2016, things were different. I was learning cognitive and communication skills. My medication for depression was working. I was hiking, meditating, doing breathwork. I was healing from the inside out. So I asked Abba, "Should I buy Diane a new ring?"

Even though God already knew that relationship would not last, He said, "Do it."

Why? Because He wanted to grow my faith. He wanted to show me that when He says something, He will make it happen.

I bought the ring — and it was not cheap — but I wanted to honor Diane for standing by me when I was broken, for loving me through all of it as best she could. We were vacationing in Hawaii when I gave it to her. She loved it. And I loved giving it to her.

What I did not know was that Diane was already having an affair. Looking back, I believe she was conflicted about it. But I gave her that ring with a full heart, and she received it.

Two years later, Diane lost the ring.

I was upset. But I brought it to God. "Abba, I love you, and I forgive Diane for losing the ring."

God said, "The ring will come back to you."

I didn't ask any more questions. I had faith. I believed. And then I let it go.

After we filed for divorce, I moved out and Amanda moved in. Then COVID-19 hit, and my income disappeared. My little pet product company had run on farmers' markets, and when the country shut down, so did everything I had built. Even through the heartbreak, I tried to show compassion. Diane and I still had to stay in touch because of our animals and the business.

One day, she called. "Fenix, move back in with me and Amanda. It's still your home. Besides, Marley and Teddy will be happy to be together again."

I asked God for guidance. He said, "Yes, move back in."

Looking back, I see exactly what He was doing.

One afternoon, Amanda came home with her bicycle. "I've got a flat tire," she said, heading toward one of the guest bedroom closets to look for a pump.

She went quiet for a moment.

Then she came running into the living room. "Fenix — I think I found your ring."

She placed it in my hand.

I was speechless. I sat there on the couch staring at it, all kinds of emotions moving through me at once. Amanda's phone rang.

"Hey, Diane." She glanced at me. "She's sitting right here. Let me pass you the phone."

"I heard Amanda found the ring," Diane said. "Did she give it to you?"

"Yes," I said. "I don't know what to say. I'm in shock."

"You said God told you He would return it to you, Fenix. It's yours. It's only right."

I took the ring to my room, shut the door, and sat in my office chair. Tears fell. That ring was a symbol of a marriage that had broken. But it was also a promise fulfilled by God — placed directly into my hands, exactly as He had said.

On that day, my faith grew from the size of a mustard seed into a mountain.

Before you turn the page, I want to say something directly to the straight reader who has stayed with me this far. This chapter was not only written for the LGBTQ+ community. It was written for every person who has ever been handed a Bible as a weapon instead of a gift. For every person who walked out of a church wounded and never went back. For every person who stopped believing God loved them because of something a human being said from a pulpit. For every person who has felt too broken, too sinful, too damaged, or too far gone to be worthy of divine love. That is who this book was written for. That is who God has been looking for all along. And if that is you — welcome. You are exactly where you are supposed to be.

Abba loves you so much. If you feel broken right now, know that God is there — waiting for you, ready to love you, laugh with you, and heal every area of your life. He doesn't ask you to be perfect first. He doesn't ask you to have it all figured out. He just asks you to open your hand.

Meet God in your heartbreak. Meet Him in your questions. Meet Him in your confusion. Meet Him in your healing. Not because you've earned it — but because that is simply who He is.

Love.

Only Love.

> **A Moment for Reflection**
> When someone uses Scripture to diminish you, can you stand grounded in the truth that Jesus's greatest commandment was always love?

Chapter 10

God Provides

"A righteous man regardeth the life of his beast:
but the tender mercies of the wicked are cruel."
—Proverbs 12:10 (KJV)

I want to share a love story about our pets.

A righteous person treats animals with compassion. Yet sometimes when people are broken, they don't treat animals kindly. When I was broken and lost, my heart could not love anything. Poppi, Marley, and Teddy all showed me love anyway. I attribute much of my healing to them. Animals are so forgiving. I believe they were put on this earth to mimic God's unconditional love.

If you are in pain right now, please don't take it out on your pet. They mean only to love you and help you heal. If you have hurt an animal, pause, ask for forgiveness, and honestly consider whether that animal might be better cared for by someone who can give it what it deserves.

God listens to us all the time. He is listening everywhere, always, at once. And sometimes — as you are about to see — He listens through the eyes of a dog.

Storytime: Marley and Marlee

It was November 2020. I was divorced. Marley, my emotional support buddy, and I were living in our apartment. I loved his big brown eyes and his even bigger heart. He was a major reason I healed. Everywhere I went, he went. He was eleven years old now, and he could no longer walk. I had bought him a doggy wheelchair, paid for acupuncture for his hip pain, and given him medication and CBD. I massaged him daily, hoping to ease what I could.

One evening, I was eating dinner when he barked — calling me to him. I got up, knelt down, and said, "You in pain, boy?" He blinked. I had taught him to blink intentionally to say yes. "Let me get you some medication." After I gave him his meds, he looked at me, pressed his snout gently against my mouth, and began to bark softly — as if he was trying to tell me something.

I stopped him. "Marley," I said quietly, "do you need help passing on? Is the pain that much for you?"

He blinked.

Tears welled in my eyes. "Okay. Let me call the vet tomorrow." He cocked his head and stared at me with so much love. "Marley," I whispered, "our job together isn't finished. I need you with me. So will you do me a favor? Promise me — come back to me. Find me. Come back as a little girl dog, a smaller breed." He blinked. I held him close and went to bed.

Before I continue, I need to tell you how Marley and I found each other — because the beginning of our story was not pretty, and I want to be honest with you about that.

He came into my life in 2011 when Diane sent me to pick up a puppy for her. I didn't even want a dog in the house. But wouldn't you know it — he ended up being my dog and my best friend. For the first two years, I provided only the basics: food, water, potty time. I was in too much emotional pain to truly love anything. I didn't know how.

Then one day, when Marley turned two, I took him to a dog park. A pit bull attacked him — fast, aggressive, relentless. I couldn't stop it. The other owner couldn't stop it. Marley was screaming, and I was screaming, grabbing at him, terrified. When it was finally over, I scooped him up and raced to the vet.

We sat together in that exam room, waiting. I looked down into his eyes. Tears were streaming down my face. In that moment I realized — I could have lost him. And I realized something else: I loved him. I got down on both knees, my voice trembling, and I made him a promise.

"From this day on, you are my dog and I am going to protect you, and you are going to protect me. I am a survivor — and now so are you. I promise I will never let anyone, or any dog, ever hurt you again."

For the first time, I caressed his face, kissed the top of his head, and gave him the biggest hug of his life. And for the first time, I gave my heart away — and it was to my dog Marley.

That was how we bonded. He became my emotional support dog and we were inseparable. He became the face of my company — his photo was on every product, he was my social media front man, and we were on the news twice. People came to my farmers' market stall and asked, "Is Marley here?" He was always lounging behind my table, and families would wait in line just to take pictures with him. Everyone loved Marley.

When it was time for Marley to cross the rainbow bridge on November 11th, 2020, I called my vet and Diane. They both came over to help me let him go. I held his frail body in my arms, kissing his face, telling him over and over, "I love you so much, Marley boy." He was ready. My vet gave him the injection and he passed quickly and peacefully.

I wailed. My heart was broken open.

For the next five months, all I did was cry. I couldn't work. I couldn't breathe without him. Friends said, "Find another dog." I said, "I only want Marley." Then one evening, a friend called. "Fenix, come paddleboarding with me and a group of friends. You need to get out." I knew she was right. I needed to live, even without him.

What happened that night I could not have scripted.

It was May 4th, 2021. There were ten of us paddling in the ocean near SeaWorld. It was evening, and fireworks started going off across the water. Everyone stopped paddling to record them on their phones. The water was perfectly calm. No wind at all.

Suddenly, my board began to drift. Out of ten boards, only mine moved. I wasn't paddling — I was holding my camera — but still, I drifted far from the group. It was dark. I couldn't see anything in the water around me.

Then I heard it — scratching on the underside of my board.

I pointed my phone light down into the water and found a drowning dog.

I shoved my phone in my pocket, reached down, and grabbed the only part of her I could catch — the top of her head. I screamed for everyone to come help. In about three minutes, the group surrounded me. I handed the dog to the board that had two riders on it, and we all paddled back to shore.

My friends handed me a soaking wet, shaking Shih Tzu with a little pink flower on her head. "She's got a collar," they said. "Her name is Bella."

I thought, *I'll keep her.* But that was not God's plan. Bella had a phone number on her tag. Her owners were staying in an RV on the other side of the bay. When they came running down the beach toward us, I held Bella wrapped in a warm towel and said what needed to be said. "You should be ashamed of yourselves. You were watching fireworks and you didn't secure your dog? She ran into the ocean. If I had not spotted her, she would have drowned."

They apologized profusely. And then their little girl — about ten years old — rushed toward me with tears streaming down her face. "Thank you for saving my dog."

I handed Bella over. "Do better," I said to her parents, as they walked away.

I believe God used Bella as a timed blessing for me. That adventure cracked my heart back open. And the very next morning, I said, "Abba, I'm ready for another dog."

I researched rescues and applied for a little white puppy. They loved my application but told me there were two people ahead of me. They promised to call when another puppy came available.

That same evening, I received a text with a photo — a tiny, two-week-old, black female pit bull mix, staring straight into the camera as if to say, *Momma, it's me.*

She had the same big brown eyes as Marley boy. I could feel her spirit calling me. I texted back immediately: *Yes. I want her.*

She had been found in a dumpster — sick, fragile, filled with worms and parasites, thrown away like trash. But the city had installed warm body detectors to stop animals from being killed that way, and because of those detectors, she was saved.

A week passed and my phone didn't ring. Then I heard God say clearly, *"Marlee is ready to be picked up. Call in the morning."* I set my alarm for the moment the rescue opened.

When the nurse answered, I said, "Hi — I'm calling to check on Marlee girl. How is she doing?"

The nurse said, "The vet just cleared her to go into a foster home."

"Can I be her foster until I can adopt her?"

"Yes, you can."

"I'm on my way."

It was May 11th, 2021. I walked through that door knowing I was not leaving without her.

The moment she heard me come in — this tiny two-week-old puppy — she ran to the edge of her soft kennel and stared at me with her big brown eyes, as if she already knew me. She couldn't take her eyes off me. And I couldn't take mine off her. Black with a white chest, big pointy ears, little white socks on her paws.

The nurse said, "Gosh — it's as if she knows you. You're meant for each other."

"I know," I said. "She's my Marlee." Her ears perked up the moment I said her name.

I picked her up, brought her snout to my face, and she ripped off my mask with her tiny paws and started kissing my face.

There was another puppy — also found in the dumpster with Marlee, a little chihuahua mix. I couldn't leave her behind. I took them both home. I called the chihuahua Zaya and promised the rescue I would foster her until a home was found.

The day they came home, Marlee was running around my apartment. I looked at her and said, "If you're Marley, look at me and blink."

She stopped playing. Sat down. Looked directly at me.

And blinked.

Then she took off like a rocket, back to jumping around with Zaya. I wailed — knowing in my bones what God had done for me.

I played a game with her to be sure. I hid while she played. Then I called, "Marlee!" That tiny three-week-old puppy stopped, turned, and came running straight to me. She knew her name. She knew *me.*

I was completely in love.

I asked God one evening, "Abba — is this my boy Marley?"

God said, "No, it's a new Marlee. Marley is with me. I sent her for you."

Even as I write this, my eyes fill with tears. I closed them, squeezed the tears away, and said, "Abba, how's Marley boy?"

God said, "Fenix-cita, why do you cry? He's with me — running, playing with his pals, eating to his heart's desire, loving his life."

If there is anything in my life I could go back and change, I wish I had loved Marley better from the very beginning. I wish I had never taken him to that dog park. But that is not how it turned out. Marley is with God. And I have a new Marlee — my little girl.

I am always amazed at how the universe unfolds for our highest good. If God had not inspired my friend to invite me paddleboarding, or if I had said no, Marlee girl would have gone to another family and lived another life. But I listened. And just at the right time, she came to me — as a little girl and a smaller breed — exactly as I had asked.

God was listening.

Am I ashamed to say I love Marlee more fully than I was able to love Marley boy? No. There is no shame in that. I love her with my whole healed heart. From the day I brought her home, she has had 100 percent of my attention and my love. I trained her from the beginning with gentleness and positive reinforcement. She was also trained by a police dog trainer — not for protection, but to make sure she is calm and compliant enough to go everywhere with me as my service dog.

Do I take her to dog parks? Absolutely not. Never.

We have traveled across the United States by car together, exploring this beautiful country. When I speak on stages, she is right there with me. When I travel by plane, she is at my feet. She gets massages, supplements, her teeth brushed, and a monthly Banfield Pet Care membership so her medical needs are always covered. She gets toys, treats, human-grade food, and all my kisses and hugs until she says — in her own way — "No more, Mom." Which is never.

Since she couldn't quite master blinking the way Marley did, she communicates by double-tapping both paws on the floor. When she wants a treat, fresh water, or a walk, she comes and stares at me and taps until I respond. It is the cutest thing I have ever seen in my life. She knows she is adorable, and she uses it shamelessly.

She makes me laugh every single day. We pray together. She cuddles in my arms every night. She jumps into the shower with me because she loves the hot water and her loofah and her gentle baby shampoo. She is my boo, and she knows it.

Let me share one more story about Marlee — a recent one.

It was December 3rd, 2025. Marlee and I flew to Florida for a speaking engagement. She was sitting in my lap on the plane when a flight attendant approached us. I thought she was going to ask me to put Marlee on the floor.

Instead she said, "Miss, I need your dog's help. We have a woman in the back having a major panic attack. We told her your dog is on the plane — her vest says 'Free Hugs' and 'Rub My Belly.' Would you and Marlee come help her?"

"This is Marlee's job," I said. "She is here to love on everyone."

We were escorted to the back of the plane, where Marlee gave that woman kisses and warmth for the entire flight. The woman stayed calm because Marlee was with her. When we landed, we were showered with a thank-you card, food, snacks, beverages, and airline miles. The flight attendants took photos with Marlee and covered her in kisses.

This is who she is. Everywhere we go, she heals people. She is God's little ambassador — a walking, tail-wagging reminder that love is always available, always free, and always exactly what people need.

Our favorite thing to do together is hike. She has carried that legacy forward — just like Marley boy did with me in San Diego. Sometimes she gets tired on the trail — she is too small and short-legged to be a pit bull mix, and it is the funniest thing — so I scoop her up, strap her over my shoulders, and we finish together. When we get home, I draw her a warm bath. She lies down in it and closes her eyes.

I always tell her, "Marlee, you owe me twenty-plus years of your life. Live for me as long as you can, okay, baby?" She listens, then double-taps her paws. *You got it, Mom.*

Every single day, I thank God for her. Not one moment goes by that I take her for granted.

If there is a lesson here for you, it is this: love your pets. The more you love them, the more love flows back to you. Protect them. Feed them well. Hold them close and thank God for them. They have done nothing but offer you unconditional love since the day they arrived in your life.

God does wonders when we let Him show us His love — and sometimes He shows it through a tiny black puppy with big brown eyes and white socks on her paws, found in a dumpster, waiting to find her way home to you.

Marlee is God's love made visible in my life. She is my blessing, my best friend, my soul mate, and my greatest daily reminder that God provides — always, in the most unexpected and beautiful ways.

I have so many more stories to share. Let's keep going.

> **A Moment for Reflection**
> Have you ever received unconditional love from an unexpected source, and recognized in that moment the quiet hand of God providing exactly what you needed?

Chapter 11
Becoming Christlike

"Let him who seeks continue seeking until he finds.
When he finds, he will become troubled.
When he becomes troubled, he will be astonished,
and he will rule over the All."
—Gospel of Thomas, Saying 2

What follows is a deeply personal spiritual experience. I share it not to elevate myself, but to show how easily awakening can be misunderstood without humility, discernment, and support.

Before I begin, I want you to sit with that passage from the Gospel of Thomas — because I have lived it, line by line, and I want you to understand what you are about to read.

"Let him who seeks continue seeking until he finds." This is the invitation to spiritual persistence. Don't stop searching for truth until you experience it directly. This isn't about intellectual curiosity — it's about inner revelation. The truth of God isn't found through half-hearted effort. It's discovered through longing, surrender, and continual seeking. Jesus said the same thing in Matthew: *"Ask, and it shall be given you; seek, and ye shall find; knock, and it shall be opened unto you"* (Matthew 7:7, KJV).

"When he finds, he will become troubled." This is where the passage gets raw and real. Finding the truth is not comfortable — it shatters illusions. When you truly encounter the divine within, your ego trembles. The old identity built on fear, control, and

separation begins to crumble. You realize that much of what the world taught you was upside down. That recognition is deeply disturbing, because awakening always disrupts comfort first. This stage is necessary. It is a spiritual detox.

"When he becomes troubled, he will be astonished." After the ego's unraveling comes awe. Once the old illusions fall away, you see reality as it truly is — radiant, interconnected, alive with divine presence. You recognize God in everything, including yourself. This is what mystics call *gnosis* — not knowledge of facts, but direct knowing of truth.

"And he will rule over the All." You become the master of your own mind, your emotions, your reactions. You live in harmony with the universe rather than being ruled by it. This is Christ consciousness realized — divine awareness that reigns not through control, but through love.

I have lived every line of this scripture. The search for truth first shook everything I believed. It disturbed me deeply, because I had to let my old self die. But on the other side of that disturbance came astonishment — the realization that the light I had been searching for was within me all along.

I need to tell you one more thing before this story begins. For a few years, I did not want to believe in Jesus. Christians had told me I was condemned — that someone like me could not have a relationship with Him. So I pushed Jesus away and held on only to God the Father. But God, being the Father of Jesus, needed me to see the truth about His Son. I believe He allowed what you are about to read for two reasons: to show me that God and Jesus are one, and to show me who I truly am through Him.

What followed was the strangest, most humbling, most hilarious year of my spiritual life.

Storytime: I Was Jesus for a Year . . . Or So I Thought

The year was 2017. I was doing the work — praying and meditating daily, doing breathwork, journaling, attending therapy, receiving EMDR to heal old trauma. I loved Diane more. I loved Marley boy. I had no more rage or anger. I responded to people with gentleness and calm. I was transforming.

And then God decided it was time to show me something.

In March of that year, I drove out of town to receive a speaking award at a nonprofit that supports people living with mental illness. That morning, I woke up early to pray and meditate. My alarm went off. I jumped in the shower. I said out loud, "I love you, Abba!"

Then God spoke: *"Kneel and pray."*

"Yes, Lord." I knelt down in the shower and prayed — giving thanks, giving gratitude, giving everything I had.

After a few minutes, God said, *"Now rise."*

I stood up.

"Now look up."

I lifted my face and raised my hands. "I love you, God!"

And then it happened.

God said, *"You are now blessed with the Holy Spirit. Know that there will be those who form against you. Know that I am always with you. I will never leave you nor forsake you."*

In that moment, I felt God breathe His Spirit into my body. An energy shock moved through me. I gasped. I crossed my arms and held myself, crying, feeling an overwhelming, radiant love enter every cell of my being.

I called Diane immediately after. She cried with me. She knew I could hear God. She knew something real was happening to me.

But then — something strange began.

I didn't understand it at the time. I do now. What happened next was my time in the desert. I was being challenged, and because I had never truly studied Scripture, I had no framework to understand what was happening to me. Something deep within me began to convince me that I was the reincarnation of Jesus.

I told Diane, "I'm Jesus. I'm the second coming of Christ."

She listened carefully and suggested I seek help.

I hired a past-life regressionist. She invited me to her home — a lovely place filled with statues of Jesus and the Buddha — and led me into a deep hypnotic trance in a quiet guest room.

I felt myself drift into another awareness entirely. I looked down and saw a long linen tunic reaching below my knees, and ancient sandals on a man's feet — my feet — walking along a dusty road. Then I saw a wooden table surrounded by men in tunics and cloaks. There was food, and I felt myself dipping bread into a sauce and eating it, speaking with the man beside me. Out of the corner of my eye, one man rose from the table and left the room. *Was that Judas?* I'll never know.

Then I was pulled upward, out of the body, and I looked down on a hillside — a scene I would later recognize, when I saw it recreated in a film, as Golgotha, the Hill of the Skull. I caught my breath in that theater. That was the moment I understood what I had witnessed.

In that same regression, I also saw Jesus — as Him, through His eyes — enter heaven. Moses was there, and he placed his hand on Jesus's heart in comfort.

I woke up and looked at the regressionist. "Am I Jesus?"

She gave me a gentle, skeptical look. She was a lovely woman in her seventies with white hair and a kind face. I don't think she believed I was Jesus. I can't say I blamed her.

That experience weighed on me heavily, because I did not *want* to be Jesus. It felt narcissistic. I woke up the next morning, emailed her, and told her: "I'm not the reincarnation of Jesus!" She invited me back to her home, and sitting beside a statue of Jesus in her living room, she said, "Fenix, I don't know why you experienced this, but I think you will discover for yourself what God is showing you."

I went home confused.

I took Diane to an Indian restaurant, ordered naan with hummus, and dipped the bread dramatically. "I'm the reincarnation of Jesus, Diane. I saw myself dipping bread, just like this." She stared at me. She wanted to help. She found videos of a man in Australia claiming to be Jesus. He was a fraud, and I knew it instantly. She found another man living in the mountains of Colorado who believed in aliens and also claimed to be the second coming. No.

"Diane," I said one afternoon, "what if you're Mary — here to help me discover who I am?"

She looked at me with the patience of a saint. "I'm not Mary, Fenix."

I was very, very wrong. But it got worse.

One afternoon, I was outside talking to God and I said, "Prove to me I'm Jesus."

God said, *"Go to the mirror."*

I walked to the bathroom and saw a bright golden aura surrounding my head. I tried to touch it — my hands went right through it. I stood there for five minutes saying, "Oh my God. What do I do with this?" Then I stumbled out of the bathroom, overwhelmed.

Over the following weeks, I would sit Diane down on the couch when she came home from work. "Diane, I have a message for the world. I'm the second coming of Christ. God is using me. Please believe me."

I'm fairly certain she was reconsidering every life decision she had ever made.

I couldn't fully believe it myself either. So I did the only thing that made sense: I called a psychologist.

The receptionist got me in that same morning. My new therapist was of medium height, thin build, wearing checkered black-and-white pants and a white blouse, her long blonde hair framed by glasses with black frames. Loving quotes about God and the Buddha covered her office walls.

She was typing while I talked. I put my hand up to stop her.

"Please stop typing and look at me when I am talking. I'm the reincarnation of Jesus. I need help."

She put her hands in her lap, looked directly at me, and said, "It's okay. Something is happening. You're having a spiritual experience, and we are going to work through it together."

She was my therapist for the next four years.

For months, the feeling persisted. I prayed, meditated, and read everything I could find. I found communities of people who understood Christ consciousness — but the moment any of them started gathering disciples, I ran. That is a cult, and I don't do cults.

Then, gradually, the feeling passed. And after four long months of silence, God spoke to me again.

"Why were you so silent, Abba?"

"I knew you would get it," He said. *"I was letting you work through this. I never left you. I was leading you toward the truth of who you are."*

"Who am I?"

"My life flows through you. You live in me. We are united in love."

"Who is Jesus?"

"He lives in you. You live in me. We are all one in love, made in my image. I am the Christ. I am God. I am the Creator."

"Are you saying I'm the actual Jesus?"

"No," He said gently. *"I am saying you are in the body of Christ."*

"The body of Christ — but not Jesus?"

"Correct. You are not Jesus, but you participate in the same divine love that lived through Him. Many are called; few choose to live from that place. You, Fenix-cita, chose to be one with me. I know your heart. I know your sincerity. You have been, and will continue to be, transformed to live as a living expression of Christ on Earth."

"What is my purpose?"

"To remind people who they are: united in love, rooted in divine truth, called to love one another as I have loved you."

"Am I meant to replace Jesus?"

"No. You are a living Christ made visible through humanity."

"So . . . is Jesus coming back?"

"Yes," He said. *"So keep your lamp ready."*

"I'm scared."

"I am with you."

"Okay."

If you are wondering whether this will happen to you — the answer is no. I say that with confidence. What happened to me occurred because I had never opened a Bible and had no understanding of what spiritual awakening looked like in Christ. If I had known Scripture, what I experienced would have felt natural and familiar rather than disorienting. But that was not my path, and God used it anyway.

What I now understand is this: I am not Jesus. But I am in the body of Christ — and so are you. When we choose to live from love, to surrender our ego, to walk as Jesus walked, we become living expressions of Christ on Earth. Jesus told us this Himself: *"That they all may be one; as thou, Father, art in me, and I in thee, that they also may be one in us."* (John 17:21, KJV)

"He that believeth on me, the works that I do shall he do also; and greater works than these shall he do." (John 14:12, KJV)

"Christ in you, the hope of glory." (Colossians 1:27, KJV)

These scriptures are not about one man in history. They are an invitation — to every human being — to become one with the love that created them.

If I had not let my ego die, if I had not sought help, if I had held on to the idea that I was the second coming — God could never have used me to deliver this message. I would have just been another person standing on a street corner, telling the world I was Jesus. And the world has enough of those.

Instead, I became something far more useful: a person who knows she is deeply loved by God, called to remind others of the same truth.

What does it feel like to live from that place? It feels like pure love. Like authority that comes not from ego but from surrender. Like knowing — in your bones — that you are here to go out into the world and share God's love.

So really, nothing changed. Except that my ego died. And I was reborn.

That is what it means to become Christlike. And it is available to every single one of us.

> **A Moment for Reflection**
> Are you willing to keep seeking even when what you find first is discomfort, knowing that on the other side of that trouble is astonishment and wholeness?

Chapter 12

God in the Cabin

"The kingdom is inside of you, and it is outside of you.
When you come to know yourselves, then you will become known,
and you will realize that it is you who are the sons
of the living Father."
—Gospel of Thomas, Saying 3

What follows is a deeply personal spiritual experience. I share it not to elevate myself, but to describe how I understood God's guidance during a season of surrender, healing, and discernment.

There are moments in life when God doesn't whisper. He interrupts.

At least that's how it felt to me. Looking back, I now see this season as the doorway into the most profound spiritual formation of my life. I thought God was moving me to recover from the divorce, from losing Marley boy, from selling and closing my company, Marley's Planet. What I came to understand was that God had stripped my life bare so He could rebuild me from the inside out. He wasn't punishing me. He was allowing everything that no longer served me to fall away, so that what remained was only what was real.

What began as loneliness, confusion, and wandering would become a sacred encounter that changed the trajectory of my soul forever. This is the story of how God led me into the mountains of Colorado Springs, into isolation, and what He said to me there in the dark.

This was my burning-bush moment.

It was June 2021. I was fully divorced. My business was gone. I was stuck, bored, and alone — but I had my little girl, Marlee. The farmers' market had reopened with COVID restrictions, and it had been a slow day. When I dragged myself home with almost everything I had brought, I flopped down on the couch, exhausted.

God said, *"Fenix-cita. Sell your business."*

"Why?" I asked.

Silence.

I looked over at a set of angel cards a friend had gifted me — she didn't know I don't practice fortune telling, and I want to be clear: I don't. I understand that divination is something to approach with caution. But in that moment, I thought, *God's gone for coffee and I need an answer.* I believe God is above all things and can work through unconventional means when He chooses to.

I shuffled the deck with one hand, slapping the cards against my palm. "Do you want me to sell the business?" I asked. The "YES" card flew out mid-shuffle. I wasn't convinced. I picked it up, stuck it back in the middle of the deck, set the whole stack down on my bed, and went to the bathroom. One minute later, I walked back in.

The "YES" card was face up. Looking right at me.

"Okay, Abba," I said. "Let's sell the business."

I called Bill and Sheila — a middle-aged couple who had purchased my dog beer for resale for years. "I know you love my dog beer company," I told them, "and I will sell it to you, as long as you leave Marley on the bottles and honor his legacy." They didn't want the treats or the food — but the beer? They were ecstatic. Within a month, the transfer was done.

I was free. No business. No Marley boy. No spouse. Nothing holding me back.

Then God spoke again.

"Fenix-cita, take Marlee girl and take a trip."

"Where to?"

"Anywhere. Go everywhere."

I packed our bags, loaded up my SUV, and we hit the road.

We drove north from California through Oregon and Washington, then across the country — Montana, Idaho, Kentucky, New York, Florida. I know the Motel 6's from coast to coast. At every stop, Marlee and I would freshen up and head out for an adventure — farmers' markets, jazz in the park, national parks, waterfalls, tourist spots, diners. In the evenings, I'd get dressed up, put Marlee in her cutest outfit with her little jewelry, settle her into her stroller, and we'd go find a fancy dinner. Strangers invited us to join them constantly. They bought us meals and spent hours with us. The love we received along that road was something I will never forget.

People asked us everywhere we went, "Where are you both headed?"

"I don't know," I'd say. "God asked me to take a trip. I recently got divorced, lost my dog, closed my company, and now I'm just going." Every single time — state after state, stranger after stranger — they would say the same thing: *I think God is getting ready to move you. I don't think California is your home anymore.*

God was planting seeds through the mouths of people I had never met before and would never see again.

One month into our travels, my friend Harmony asked me to come to Indiana to officiate her wedding. I signed up for an officiant certificate through the Universal Life Church that same day — and just like that, I became Reverend Fenix. I wore all white: white blouse, white blazer, white jeans, white shoes. Marlee wore her little gold chain and a white t-shirt that read: *"My mommy is a single hottie lesbian."* Harmony wore a beautiful white dress, and her beau, Elijah, wore a black and gold African dashiki kaftan. The handfasting ceremony was held in a hotel ballroom decorated with white lilies and white tablecloths. I presented the service they had written, they spoke their vows, and it was short, sweet, and deeply romantic. I was honored to be part of their day.

That night, I went back to the hotel and fell asleep.

At 3:00 a.m., God woke me up.

"Fenix-cita, you are moving to Colorado."

I opened my eyes, looked at my phone. 3:00 a.m. "I am? Okay, Abba. Goodnight." And I went back to sleep.

In the morning I said, "Marlee, let's go. Colorado!" And we drove.

As we approached Denver on the freeway, a moment of fear hit me. *Why do I have to move?* In that exact instant, I saw a neon sign on a Ford dealership billboard: *"I know you're afraid. Do it anyway."*

That was all I needed. I changed my thoughts to God's thoughts and said, "Marlee, let's check out our new home." I spent three glorious days exploring Denver and left ready to sell my furniture and sever every tie to California.

The night before I headed home, God woke me at 3:00 a.m. again. *"Book an Airbnb in Colorado Springs."* I grabbed my phone, opened the app, found a cabin, booked it, and went back to sleep. By this point, I had learned to move quickly with God. Hesitation only creates confusion.

I moved into the Colorado Springs cabin in September 2021. Mountains. Deer. Black bears. Crisp air that made you feel like you were breathing for the first time. It was stunning.

And I was completely alone.

Why am I here? I was lonely, confused, and isolated. God even said, *"Delete your social media."* Not deactivate — delete. I deleted fifteen years of my life from social media: photos, memories, connections, all of it. Gone. I did it without hesitation. I want to be clear that this was specific guidance for my own season of healing — not universal instruction for everyone. But for me, in that moment, it was right.

The weeks passed slowly. The silence was heavy. I was not giving myself any grace.

One evening, I called on God. "Who is my wife? You said you have someone for me." Nothing. Three hours later, I tried again. "What is my purpose? Tell me about that." Still nothing. Six more hours of silence, and I had worked myself into a full-blown frenzy.

I found a cabin online for $150,000. "Fine," I said to God. "I'll buy this cabin and become a hermit. I'll get a job as a clerk. Forget this divine spiritual calling you have for my life." I was furious. And then — because I am nothing if not honest — I said, "You know what, God? If you're going to ignore me, I'm going to go get a marijuana joint, smoke it, and then you can be mad at me."

And I did it. I drove to a marijuana store like the rebellious child I apparently still was, bought one joint and a black Bic lighter, and drove back to the cabin.

I share this not to glorify rebellion, but because this is who I was in that moment — human, frustrated, sincere, and absolutely at the end of my rope. Faith does not mean the absence of frustration. Sometimes it means doing what you need to do to surrender, even if the path there is messy.

I came home, lit a two-wick candle that was already melted more than half way down the jar, closed all the windows, turned off the lights, and sat down in the living room. *Time to relax.* I grabbed the lighter and flicked it. In an instant, God ejected every last drop of gas from the lighter in one whoosh — then blew out the flame, no more gas, nothing. Empty.

I knew immediately it was God.

"Oh yeah?" I said out loud. "I have a candle lit."

I stood up and reached toward the candle jar to use the flame to light my joint. Before my hand could reach it, God blew out the candle.

The room was dark. And I felt His presence — a tangible, unmistakable energetic weight, concentrated in one spot in that room, as if He wanted me to know exactly where He was standing.

I sat back down on the couch. "Yes, Lord," I said, as humbly as I could manage.

And then God spoke — not as a demand, but as an invitation. Three things: *"Rebuild my church. Leave a legacy for me in your name. Your wife is twin flame."*

Then silence. His presence left.

I did not smoke that joint. I knelt down and I prayed.

What God Said — and What He Meant

Let me take you through those three directives, because they changed the entire direction of my life.

"Rebuild my church." When most people hear the word *church*, they picture a building. But the original Greek word is *Ekklesia*, which means "gathering" or "community." God was not asking me to construct an institution or start a religion. He was asking me to help people rediscover authentic relationship with Him — outside of fear, outside of dogma, outside of the walls that religion had built around His love. The rebuilding began inside me first. The true church is every heart where God dwells. To rebuild the church meant to start with myself — clear the clutter, heal the wounds, make room for love — and then let that healing spread naturally to others. That is what this book is.

"Leave a legacy for me in your name." God was not asking me to make my name famous. He was asking me to make His love unforgettable through my life. A legacy is not a monument — it is a mirror. It is living in such a way that when people remember your name, they remember how safe they felt, how seen, how healed, how hopeful. The legacy was never about me. It always pointed back to Him.

"Your wife is twin flame." When God said *twin flame*, I did not hear it the way modern spirituality often describes it — obsession, completion, romantic destiny. I heard it as refinement. As Scripture says, iron sharpens iron. What God was showing me was not a person to chase, but a kind of sacred partnership — two souls aligned in mutual surrender to God, growing together in service, love, and purpose. When love enters my life again, it will be a divine reflection: two souls with matching fire, called to build something blessed together. It was less about finding the one, and more about becoming the one.

Called and Chosen

That night in the cabin marked the end of my search for external answers. God had been silent for six hours not because He wasn't there, but because He was preparing me to listen differently. He had to empty me of expectation before He could fill me with revelation.

The voice of God does not come when you demand it. It comes when you surrender enough to hear it.

Jesus said in Matthew 22:14 (KJV): *"For many are called, but few are chosen."*

I used to hear that as God playing favorites. Now I hear it as an invitation to free will.

The call is universal — that quiet tug inside that says, *Wake up. Come home. Step into your true self.* Every human being hears it through conscience, through longing, through experience. But the chosen are not hand-selected by God. The chosen are the ones who *choose back.* They accept the invitation. They do the inner work. They put on what the parable calls the wedding garment — the symbol of readiness, humility, and transformation.

To be chosen is to choose yourself. To say yes to growth, to healing, to alignment with love — even when it is hard, even when God has been silent for six hours and you are sitting in a dark cabin in Colorado with an unlit joint in your hand.

The call comes from God. But the response must come from you.

The Kingdom of Heaven is within you. It has always been within you. *"Seek, and ye shall find; knock, and it shall be opened unto you"* (Matthew 7:7, KJV).

Go within. That is where God is waiting.

> **A Moment for Reflection**
> What if the losses you are grieving right now are not punishments, but God clearing space to rebuild you into something truer and stronger?

Chapter 13

What God Showed Me About the Cross

"Go within yourself; go with love."
—The Book of Thomas the Contender

For a long time, I searched for forgiveness as something to understand rather than something to receive. I studied Scripture, ancient texts, and the teachings of Jesus, and I saw clearly that He forgave freely — often instantly — meeting people exactly where they were. He did not wait for perfection before offering mercy. He spoke forgiveness as love in motion.

But God gently showed me that forgiveness does not stop there.

The cross did not replace forgiveness. It revealed the depth of it.

Jesus did not go to the cross because God was withholding mercy. He went because love was willing to remain present even in suffering. The cross is not a transaction to be analyzed — it is a revelation to be received. It shows us what love looks like when it is pushed to its absolute edge and still refuses to become hate.

When Jesus was on the cross, He said, *"Father, forgive them; for they know not what they do"* (Luke 23:34, KJV). He was not teaching a doctrine. He was embodying divine love. Forgiveness was not something He waited to give — it was who He was, even in agony.

What God showed me is this: forgiveness begins within us, but the cross teaches us how far love is willing to go once it begins. It invites us not only to receive mercy, but to become merciful. Not only to be forgiven, but to forgive — especially when it costs us something.

I no longer stand at the cross to explain it. I stand there to be changed by it. And because of that, I now carry my own.

The hardest people to forgive are rarely strangers. They are the ones who were supposed to love us first.

Storytime: Healing My Relationship with My Parents

I want to be very honest in sharing this story, because it is tender — especially for anyone who has ever been estranged from a parent and wondered whether the distance was worth it, or whether the wound would ever fully close.

As you know, I left home at fourteen. For most of my life after that, I carried a question I could never quite answer: *Did my parents love me?* Their love had always felt conditional — as if loving us was more obligation than choice.

Early in this book, I shared the words that broke something in me as a child. My father's fist on the table. *"Are you a sicko lesbian?"* My mother at the bedroom door when I was trying to end my life. *"If you're going to kill yourself, do it outside. I don't want blood on my carpet."* I need to say something important here: my parents do not recall saying those words. And I believe them. I believe those moments were so painful that their minds protected them by burying the memory. People do that. Trauma does that — to everyone involved, not just the child.

Even before those moments, I remember my father sitting my siblings and me on the couch, reading the Bible aloud. His tone was authoritative — almost aggressive. What I learned in those moments was not Scripture. What I learned was fear.

Leaving home at fourteen is dangerous for any child. And they let me go. For many years, I believed that my father's decision not to fight for me shaped every hard thing that followed. I treated my parents poorly in return, and they kept their distance. Every time I visited, we argued. Every time, I left.

But something began to shift in me — slowly, quietly, the way real healing always moves.

I realized I was the one who needed to forgive. The cross showed me this — not as a weapon of guilt, but as a mirror of love. It revealed my own unhealed places and helped me see that my parents were the last people I had not truly forgiven. I was still holding a grudge, even while believing I had healed. I had done the work on almost everything else. But this — this I had been quietly carrying for thirty-five years.

In March of 2024, after five years of no contact, my sister Jane encouraged me to visit home. My father's health had been declining after a serious accident, and time suddenly felt precious in a way it hadn't before. I flew home alone, leaving Marlee behind, unsure of what might surface.

The moment I walked through the door, everything rose up at once.

I sat my parents down and told them honestly how I had felt — all of it, all those years.

"I need you to acknowledge that you weren't really there for me," I said.

My dad looked at me and said, "Fenix, we let you move out because we didn't want to control you. I thought I was doing the right thing by letting you go live your life. I truly believed I was being a good father."

Those first two days were heavy. We all walked on eggshells. The night before I was due to leave, I sat alone on the bed in their guest room and cried. And that is when the truth finally landed — quietly, the way truth usually does: *I was the one still holding the past. I was the one preventing the healing.*

That night, I went to them in tears. I told them that no matter what had happened, they were my parents and I was their daughter — and that I wanted a loving relationship with them. Not a perfect one. Not a rewritten history. Just love, moving forward. Forgiveness didn't mean excusing what happened. It meant choosing love anyway.

And I forgave them.

Five months later, I returned home with a different heart entirely. I knew that if I wanted a different relationship, it had to begin with me. I spent those days loving my parents — laughing together, cooking, watching movies, just being present. And it was beautiful. Simple and beautiful in the way only repaired things can be.

Today, I call them just to say, "I love you." I visit when I can. We stay connected across the distance in ways we never managed when I lived close by.

And my mother — the woman who once stood at that bathroom door — now says to me, "Hija, I am so proud of you. Look at all you have accomplished. You are strong, beautiful, and God has always protected you."

It took nearly thirty-five years to release the pain, the resentment, and the grief. But I released it. And what came in to fill that space was something I had been waiting for my whole life — a mother's pride, a father's peace, and the quiet, steady warmth of a family that chose to love each other anyway.

If you are estranged from your parents, I know your pain. Truly. But I also know what is waiting for you on the other side of forgiveness. I am not asking you to excuse what happened. I am asking you to consider not letting it imprison your future.

If you are a parent estranged from your child — repair it. Open your heart. Forgive, as God forgives us. The time you think you have is never as much as you believe.

And if you are the child — consider forgiving your parents. Not for them. For you.

Forgiveness starts with you. It always has.

The cross taught me that. And I am grateful — for the lesson, for my parents, and for the life they gave me.

> **A Moment for Reflection**
> Can you receive forgiveness not as something to intellectually understand, but as an act of love already extended to you — even in your worst moment?

Chapter 14

Love Even After Rejection

"He came unto his own, and his own received him not."
—John 1:11 (KJV)

Have you ever been rejected by someone you loved?

If you have, you are in good company. The entire Bible is a painful love story — God reaching toward His people again and again, and His people turning away again and again. From the very beginning, His own angels corrupted what He had made. His people became slaves. He raised up Moses to free them, and they wandered in the desert for forty years, hardening their hearts even as He provided for them daily. Time after time, story after story, God extended His love — and time after time, it was refused.

And then He came to earth in flesh. And even then, "his own received him not."

God has always known rejection. He has always loved anyway.

I wanted to know how that felt. I just didn't fully understand what I was asking for when I prayed it.

One day I said to God, "Abba, I want to love the way you love. I want to experience the love you experience."

He heard me. And He answered — in the most unexpected, painful, and beautiful way possible.

Storytime: I Want to Love the Way You Love

Let me take you back to 2019.

Diane had just asked me for a divorce. I was broken open — standing in the bathroom, tears on my face, the life I had built for fifteen years dissolving around me. And in that moment of complete emptiness, God did something I did not expect.

He showed me someone.

Not a full picture. Just enough to know. And He said, "When you see her, you will know."

I held that quietly for four years.

I moved to Denver, Colorado in early 2023. New city, new career, new chapter. I was loving life — working out, hiking with Marlee, meeting interesting people. *New town. New place. New me. Let's go.*

Then one ordinary day I walked through a door, and there she was. My soul recognized her before my mind could form a single coherent thought. My heart didn't race — it landed. Like it had been searching for somewhere to rest and had finally found it.

Is that her?

In all my years, through everything I had lived and loved and survived, I had never felt anything like this. Not with Diane. Not with anyone. This was different in a way I cannot fully put into words — like recognizing someone you have always known, in a body you are only now meeting for the first time.

We talked for an hour. I could have talked to her forever.

The circumstances were complicated. There were real, legitimate reasons why I could not simply ask her out — reasons that required patience, respect, and time. So I honored that. I showed up. I was careful with her space. And slowly, beautifully, we began to connect.

We never got to have coffee outside those walls. Never got to take a proper walk with Marlee. But inside that room, something was alive between us. Shared laughter that felt easy and familiar. She loved Marlee.

I would go home and pray with everything I had.

"God, if there was ever a woman I wanted to love, it is her. If it is your will for us to be together — bring us together."

Tears fell every single time.

I wanted to be brave. I wanted to write her a letter — just to ask if we could spend time together outside of those walls. But my fear of rejection got the better of me, and instead of sitting with the discomfort, I made a poor decision. I ate marijuana gummies before writing it, thinking it would calm my nerves. What I didn't account for was the hour it takes for them to take effect. By the time I wrote and delivered that letter, I was not myself.

I handed her the letter that day. She tucked it into her backpack, and then we talked. She told me she couldn't pursue anything for two years. It was the most clarifying and the most heartbreaking thing I had ever heard at the same time. But she could also tell something was wrong with me. She didn't know I was under the influence from those marijuana gummies.

Then she went home and read the letter.

The next time I saw her, the door was closed. She had realized, from what I had written, that I had been under the influence of something. It had turned her off completely. The version of me she met in that conversation and the version of me in that letter were not the person she had gotten to know. Big turnoff.

I found my copy the next morning and read it with sober eyes. My heart sank. It was incoherent. It was not who I am. And it had cost me something precious.

It is a mistake I have never repeated. I chose sobriety of mind from that day forward — completely and permanently.

A month later, I saw her in passing. She walked by without a word. Her silence said everything. I did not approach her. I never would. She had made her decision and I respected it fully — even though it broke my heart.

Still, I loved her.

A year later, I reached out to apologize. She responded. I told her the truth about the gummies, told her I was sorry, told her it was never who I was. She accepted the apology graciously.

And then, again, she stepped back.

I had to accept what was in front of me. She was not coming forward. The door was closed.

And I had to be okay with that.

So I said to God what I have learned to say when I cannot control the outcome: Lord I let go. If it be your will, it will be. If not, then it won't. I will always love you God.

I left behind hope.

But I carried love.

One evening not long after, I was lying in a warm bath, listening to a love song about a woman who loved someone she could never have — and loved them anyway, without condition, without possession, without end. My heart went completely quiet.

This is unconditional love, I thought. *And it is the most painful thing I have ever felt.*

"Lord," I said out loud, "remove this from me. It causes my heart so much pain."

And then God's spirit filled the room.

"This is how I love."

"I love even when I am rejected."

"I love even when my children choose to turn from me."

"I love even when I am hated and mocked."

"Fenix-cita — now you have experienced how I love."

I wept. Deeply, quietly, completely.

He had answered the prayer I prayed without understanding what I was asking. *Let me love the way you love.* God had not answered it as a concept or a teaching. He had answered it as a lived, aching, real experience — because that is the only way to truly know what unconditional love costs.

God's love is patient. It is non-forceful. It is respectful of every boundary and every closed door. It does not demand to be received. It does not stop loving simply because the love is not returned. It simply remains — steady, present, and unwilling to become something less than itself.

That is what I now carry for her.

She will never know the depth of what I felt. She wanted nothing to do with me. And I will always have love in my heart for her.

Not with longing. Not with pain. Just love — clean and quiet and without agenda.

That is what God's love looks like. And now I know what it feels like from the inside.

What Love Is

That season taught me more about love than any book or sermon ever could. So let me tell you what I now know: Love is patient. Love is kind. Love is gentle. Love can heal all wounds. Love can feel like joy — and love can, at times, feel like grief. Love restores. Love forgives. Love does not force anything. Love allows people to be exactly who they are. Love does not judge. Love does not condemn. Love frees people rather than binding them. Love does not attach to outcomes. Love lets go and still loves, even when it is not loved back.

Love does not scream. Love does not wound. Love does not tell someone their very existence is a sin. Love does not divide or destroy. Love is not violent — not with fists, not with words, not with silence used as a weapon.

Love chooses you first — so that you have something real to give.

Love is God. And God is Love.

Love Like This

I see the world in pain. I see people who are searching for God being driven away by the very people who claim to represent Him. Division is the enemy's greatest strategy — it destroys faith, cancels love, and turns hearts away from God. We were never called to fight each other.

I do not go around shouting *"Repent of your sins!"* I believe God asks us to live the message — to be graceful, to be merciful, to show people by the way we move through the world why love matters. To wake up each morning and ask God to align our thoughts with His and our hearts with His. And then to go be that.

To forgive always. To help where we can. To use our gifts for others. To love our enemies. To give thanks in all things, even when gratitude feels impossible.

That, I believe, is the life and teaching of Jesus — not a doctrine, but a way of showing up for one another.

If you have ever felt rejected, unwanted, or walked away from — God understands that pain more intimately than anyone. He loved us before we knew His name. He loves us when we ignore Him. He loves us when we deny Him. He does not demand our love in return. He simply waits — hands open, heart wide — patient beyond all human understanding.

If you allow Him fully into your life, He will become your greatest ally, your best friend, your father or mother — whatever you need most. He knows your heart. He sees your pain. He does not judge. He waits.

This is the love Jesus showed us on the cross.

This is the love that forgives seventy times seven.

This is the love that remains when human love is not returned.

May we all learn to love like this.

May we all become a safe place for others to encounter God's love.

May our lives reflect the kind of love that does not wound, divide, or condemn — but heals, restores, and welcomes.

And if nothing else, may we remember this truth: *God has never stopped loving you. Not once.*

> **A Moment for Reflection**
> Is there someone in your life you have loved without condition, without return, and without regret — and can you see now that love like that is never wasted?

Chapter 15

What Is Christ Consciousness?

Christ consciousness is not a new age concept or a made-up idea. It is an invitation — one that every human being is capable of responding to. It is the awakening to the truth that the Divine is not somewhere outside of you, waiting to be earned or found or unlocked by the right set of rules. It is within you. Flowing through every cell of your body, your soul, your mind. Right now. Already.

In this chapter we are going to explore what it means to embody Christ — and how to awaken the same divine awareness that Jesus modeled, which is available to every single person who is willing to receive it.

What Christ Consciousness Means

"Christ" is not Jesus's last name. It is a title. In Greek, *Christos* (Χριστός) means "The Anointed One" — divine awareness flowing through human form. So Christ consciousness is not a person. It is a state of being — the moment when divine love, wisdom, and unity awaken fully inside a human mind and heart.

It is what Jesus meant when He said, *"I and my Father are one"* (John 10:30, KJV). And when He said, *"The kingdom of God is within you*" (Luke 17:21, KJV). Jesus embodied that awareness so completely that He demonstrated what it looks like when humanity and divinity fully unite — and then He turned to us and said, *you can do this too.*

At its core, Christ consciousness is the realization that we are not separate from God, from one another, or from creation itself. It shows up as unconditional love — seeing all people as part of the same source. As compassion — responding to suffering with understanding rather than judgment. As presence — living fully in this moment, without the weight of fear or guilt. As wisdom — perceiving life through divine intelligence rather than ego. And as forgiveness — releasing separation, even when we have been genuinely wronged.

When this consciousness awakens in you, belief matures into lived experience. You stop believing *about* God and begin experiencing God *as* life itself.

What Jesus Modeled

Jesus didn't just teach about God. He revealed what union with God looks like in a human body. And He made it clear that the Christ — the divine awareness — is not limited to Him alone. It lives within everyone.

He said: *"He that believeth on me, the works that I do shall he do also; and greater works than these shall he do; because I go unto my Father"* (John 14:12, KJV).

That was not arrogance. That was an open invitation. He was saying — *you too can awaken the same Spirit that lives in me.* The cross, the miracles, the parables — they were never about elevating ego or demanding worship from a distance. They were mirrors, pointing inward, inviting every one of us toward transformation.

How to Awaken Christ Consciousness

There is no single path to Christ consciousness, but there are consistent inner steps that open the same door. I want to share a simple, practical framework — one I have lived myself — that can help you awaken the life of Christ within you.

But before anything else, we cannot do this alone. We must begin by inviting Jesus in.

"Dear Jesus, I invite you into my life. I choose you as my Lord and Savior, and I desire to be one with you and with God. Please open my heart and mind to be Christlike — mirroring your love and your divinity. Amen."

Now let's walk through this together.

Step 1: Silence the Noise

"Be still, and know that I am God." (Psalm 46:10, KJV)

Stillness is where everything begins. It quiets the noise of fear, distraction, and ego so we can become attentive to God's presence. Jesus withdrew to quiet places to pray — regularly, intentionally — because He understood that intimacy with God grows in silence.

Stillness can take many forms: prayer, meditation on Scripture, walking in nature, or simply sitting quietly with God and letting the noise of the day fall away. If you are new to stillness, start small. Even five minutes a day is enough to begin. What matters most is consistency, not perfection. I began this way myself over ten years ago — just a few quiet minutes each morning — and it changed everything.

After I pray, I sit quietly and place my attention on my heart, breathing slowly and allowing peace to settle. I don't force answers. I simply remain present, trusting that God hears me and will respond in His time and His way.

Here is a prayer I use that you are welcome to make your own: *"God, thank you for showing me I am worthy of love. That I am more than enough. That when the time is right, the right person will enter my life. I surrender — with faith and inner knowing that I am already held in your love."*

After that prayer, become still. Focus inward. And if you want to experience something beautiful, try this: breathe in deeply, hold it, squeeze your whole body, and release. Then tap into a feeling of love — and double it. This simple practice helps heal your nervous system, releases stuck energy, and opens your heart wider than you thought possible.

Mantra For This Step

"I am love in action.
I am worthy.
I am made perfect in the eyes of God.
I am whole and complete."

Step 2: Forgive Everything

Forgiveness is one of the hardest — and most freeing — teachings of Jesus. When we hold onto resentment, shame, or anger, those wounds continue to live inside us, quietly shaping every thought, every reaction, every relationship. Forgiveness doesn't excuse what happened. It doesn't deny the pain. It simply releases *you* from carrying it any longer.

Jesus taught us to forgive seventy times seven — not because others always deserve it, but because *your heart deserves peace.*

Here is a practice that helped me when forgiveness felt impossible:

Take a pen and paper — not a keyboard — and write down everyone who has hurt you. Write honestly. Include the betrayal, the heartbreak, the anger, the shame, the things you have been afraid to admit even to yourself. Let it all come out. This is between you and God.

Then read what you wrote. Read it again. Over time, the words begin to lose their sharp edge. The story that once controlled your emotions starts to soften.

And here is something that might surprise you — read those words aloud in a playful or exaggerated voice. The voice of a cartoon character. Mickey Mouse, if you like. It will feel silly. That is exactly the point. Humor gently disarms pain and helps your nervous system release what it has been holding. It doesn't erase the past — it helps your body stop reliving it.

Forgiveness is a process, not a single moment. And if the pain feels overwhelming or tied to deep trauma, please talk with a counselor or therapist. Seeking help is not weakness. It is wisdom — and it is one of the bravest things you can do.

Mantra For This Step

"I forgive myself.
I forgive you.
I forgive those who hurt me.
I am whole, complete, and healed.
I have forgiven all."

Step 3: See God in All Things

Christ consciousness is not about escaping the world. It is about learning to see God at work within it. Jesus taught us that the Kingdom of Heaven is not found somewhere far away — it begins within our own hearts. When our inner life is healed and rooted in love, our way of seeing everything begins to change.

Seeing God in all things does not mean pretending life is perfect or denying pain. It means choosing to look at people and circumstances through the lens of grace rather than fear. It means believing — even in difficulty, even in confusion, even in unanswered questions — that God is present and working.

For me, this began to shift as I practiced stillness and prayer. Over time, peace became more familiar to me than conflict. Not because my challenges disappeared, but because my response to them changed. When the heart is at rest, it becomes less reactive, less drawn into chaos, and more deeply grounded in trust.

Mantra For This Step

Place your hand on your heart and say —
*"I love my life. God is with me.
I choose peace over fear."*

Step 4: Choose Love over Fear

Ego speaks in fear. Spirit speaks in love. Every time you choose love — over aggression, over bitterness, over road rage, over the urge to retaliate — you strengthen the Christ awareness within you. When your thoughts and energy are aligned with God's, love wins. Jesus showed us this again and again. Love is always the higher way.

And yes — this includes driving. ☺

Mantra For The Road

*"I will arrive at my destination with peace, on time, and safely.
Everything is perfect."*

Then put on your favorite music, breathe, and don't rush. Trust that everything is unfolding exactly as it should. God wants you to arrive safely — and so do I.

Step 5: Serve

Service is love in motion. When you help, heal, or comfort others, you expand your awareness of oneness and step fully into the life Christ modeled. Open a door for someone. Help a stranded animal. Show up for someone who is struggling. Give to a cause that moves your heart — not out of obligation, but out of overflow.

You don't need to give to a church or follow anyone's rules about generosity. Just do something. One small act of kindness, offered with a full heart, ripples further than you will ever see.

Mantra For Service

"God, thank you for showing me how I can help the world today — even if it's through one small act of kindness."

The Transformation

When Christ consciousness takes root in you, fear begins to loosen its grip. Judgment fades. You start to see life through the eyes of compassion and truth. You don't become Jesus — you become rooted in Christ, awake to the divine life of God moving within you.

This happened to me. Slowly, imperfectly, beautifully — it happened.

Christ consciousness is not a religion. It is a remembrance. It is waking up to what you already are — love, living in a human body, on its way back home to God.

Jesus didn't come to make us worship Him from a distance. He came to show us what a life fully surrendered to God looks like — and to invite us into that same life. To forgive without condition. To love without limits. To refuse to see anyone as separate from God — not even yourself.

So go, my friend. Be love. Be who God created you to be. Let your light shine so brightly that He can place it on a hill and use it to help heal the world.

People around you are praying for kindness. For mercy. For hope. For someone to show them that God is real and that love is possible and that healing is not just a word.

Sometimes — you are the answer to that prayer.

Go live like it.

> **A Moment for Reflection**
> What would change in your daily life if you truly believed that the divine awareness Jesus embodied is already alive and accessible within you?

Chapter 16
Trusting the Journey

"Whoever drinks from My mouth will become like Me;
I Myself shall become that person, and the things
that are hidden will be revealed to them."
—The Gospel of Thomas, Saying 108

After my burning-bush moment in the Colorado Springs cabin, I stayed two more months and then moved into a gorgeous apartment in a gated community. High ceilings, a pool, a gym, a dog park — it had everything. Five minutes from the Garden of the Gods, a stunning city-owned park with red rock cathedral spires, hiking trails, wildlife, and wild flora that made you feel like you were standing inside a painting. Marlee and I hiked there four times a week. I meditated daily, found a loving church, worked out, and volunteered with charity organizations.

I was learning what it felt like to live in divine awareness — and the world around me was reflecting it back.

That is what happens when Christ consciousness begins to take root. Your inner life heals, and slowly, quietly, your outer life begins to reorganize itself around that healing. Relationships soften. Your home feels calmer. The people drawn to you begin to carry depth, kindness, and honesty. Opportunities feel less accidental and more guided. You stop striving to prove your worth and start living from it. Meaning is no longer something you chase — it is something you carry.

The miracle is not that life becomes perfect. It is that your eyes open to the grace already moving within it.

I was living proof of that. And God was just getting started.

Storytime: Moving to Denver

It was September 2022. I was in Colorado Springs, volunteering with NAMI — giving speeches, holding workshops, running group meetings for people living with mental illness. I didn't know it at the time, but God was using that season to prepare me for the career waiting for me in Denver.

After a year in Colorado Springs, God made it clear — it was time to move.

"But Abba," I said, "I have three months left on this lease. If I walk away I'll lose thousands of dollars."

He didn't argue with me. He just handled it.

That same week, around 10:00 p.m., I got a frantic call from my friends Max and his wife Josie. Two masked men were trying to break into their apartment. I talked them through it — lights on, stay put, call 911. The next day, too shaken to go back home, they came to stay with me. I cooked them dinner, and over the meal I asked what they planned to do.

"We can't go back there," they said.

"Do you like this apartment?"

"We love it."

"Then it's yours. Move in, take over my lease, keep my deposit. I need to get to Denver."

Within two weeks, Max and Josie were settled into that beautiful apartment — where they still live today — and I was on my way to Denver. God had put the move on my heart and then quietly arranged every detail without me even asking Him to.

I researched Denver apartments and told God exactly what I wanted. "Abba, I want sexy. A high-rise downtown with all the amenities. Flashy. In the middle of everything."

God said, *"No."*

"Alright. Where do you want me?"

"Look west. About fifteen minutes outside of Denver. You can choose from there."

I looked west and found a brand-new apartment building at Sloan's Lake — beautiful, classy, safe, everything I needed. Marlee and I were the first residents to move in.

Then one afternoon I drove through Denver to get a feel for the city. Downtown, I spotted a building with a heart as its logo. Something leapt inside me. "Abba — there. I want to work there. Open those doors."

I went home, lit a candle, put on some R&B slow jams, thanked God in advance, and looked up what positions were available. I found it immediately — Peer Support Specialist, riding with police officers, helping people who were homeless, addicted, or living with mental illness. It was exactly who I was. I applied.

A month passed. Nothing. I took a walk with Marlee and said, "Abba, if this job isn't for me, let me know. If you want me to keep resting, I'm okay with that."

The next day, they called me for an interview.

I walked in and told the hiring team, "This job is mine. You should hire me immediately." They laughed. "Where's my desk?" I asked.

I got the job.

For the next two and a half years, I worked as a clinical first responder — a Peer Support Specialist alongside the Denver Police Department. Our three-person team was called the SUN: Substance Use Navigators. We went into the roughest neighborhoods in the city and offered medical help, temporary housing, and detox opportunities to people the world had forgotten.

I have seen things in that work that I will never forget. Underground tunnels. Abandoned buildings filled with filth and hopelessness. People overdosed and frozen. I waded through mud, through trash, through the wreckage of lives that addiction had hollowed out. And in every broken face, I saw a version of the person I used to be.

I made it my quiet mission to remind people that God was still there. I prayed with them in secret, discreetly, only when they wanted it. But they never forgot me.

One of those people was Jason — a former author, once an altar boy who had been raped by a Catholic priest. The trauma drove him to drugs, homelessness, and paranoia. He was smart, kind, the kind of man any employer would have been lucky to have. But pain has a way of dismantling even the strongest people when it goes unhealed.

We lost contact for a year. Then one day, officers on my team arrested him for trespassing. He asked them, "Where's Fenix? I want to talk to Fenix."

I opened the back door of that police car and found my buddy Jason — handcuffed, despondent, eyes hollow. We hugged.

"Jason," I said, "it's now or never. You can go to jail right now, or you can let me help you."

"I'm in," he said. "I'm ready."

I had him escorted to a hotel for a week while I secured him a two-year housing voucher. In my two years with the SUN team, I helped hundreds of people like Jason find their way off the streets and toward healing. Every single one of them mattered.

But after two years of waking at 3:00 a.m., hitting the gym, working 6:00 a.m. to 4:30 p.m., and falling into bed by 7:00 p.m. every night — I was completely burned out. A new mayor had been elected with a different vision for Denver, and the approach to homelessness shifted in ways that made my work feel impossible. The city was hiding its problems rather than healing them.

I went to God. "Abba, I love you. You are my breath, my life, my father. I am so grateful for these two years. But I am exhausted. I want to give this job back to you. I need rest."

God said, *"Fenix-cita, do not turn in your two-week notice. Hold on just a little longer. It's not time."*

"Okay, Abba. I'll wait."

He showed me a vision — that I would soon be able to collect unemployment and move out of state. I held that quietly and kept showing up.

Seven months earlier, in October 2024, my job had told me I needed to use my accumulated vacation time or they would cut me a check. I took the month off with no real plan — until one of my officers suggested Texas. "Texas," I said. "Let's go."

Marlee and I packed up and spent a month exploring Dallas, Austin, and San Antonio. The hospitality, the food, the connections, the dates — I fell in love with the state completely. I came back to Denver already knowing, in my bones, that Texas was next.

Then in July 2025, Human Resources called our SUN team into the boardroom. I already knew what was coming. I rested my legs on a chair and got comfortable.

"We have difficult news," the representative said. "The City of Denver has pulled the SUN grant. You can apply for a position within the hospital or file for unemployment."

There it was. God's vision — confirmed. All I had to do was wait on Him.

I sold and gave away everything I owned — again — and moved to Houston, Texas. Living in the Lone Star State. Living my best life. And expecting more blessings, because that is simply who God is. He loves to love. He loves to give good gifts to His children. And He never — not once — runs out.

I could fill another book with stories of God working in my life. But what I really want is for you to have your own stories to tell.

Your own burning bush. Your own Max and Josie miracle. Your own building with a heart. Your own moment of waiting — and then watching God arrange every detail you couldn't have arranged yourself.

All of that is available to you. Right now. Exactly as you are.

All you have to do is open the door and let Him in.

> **A Moment for Reflection**
> Are you in a season of waiting, and can you trust that showing up faithfully in the in-between is itself the sacred work?

Chapter 17
Awakening the Christ Within

"The kingdom is inside of you and it is outside of you."
—The Gospel of Thomas, Saying 3

Let's talk.

Do you feel broken? Depressed? Angry? Have you been betrayed by someone you loved? Do you drink or use drugs to numb the pain? Are you reactive — easily offended, quick to explode, touchy behind the wheel? Do you have road rage? Have you wanted to end your life? Do you feel unloved?

I know your pain. I lived every single one of those things.

I had uncontrollable rage — in my home, in my car, around people who were only trying to love me. I know what it feels like to act in a way that says, *I am broken inside and I do not know how to fix it.* I was a drug addict and a raging alcoholic. I suffered from hypervigilance, paranoia, psychosis, and rage I could not contain. I hated who I was, how I looked, how I felt. I didn't love myself — so how could I have loved anyone else?

When we are broken inside, we cannot give what we do not have.

If any of this sounds like you, I want to say something gently but honestly: it may be wise to remain single for a season and focus on healing first. Not because you are not worthy of love — you are. But because you deserve to enter your next relationship as your whole self, not your wounded one. Heal first. Step into love regret-free.

Is there something inside you that longs for a different life? A life with deeper peace, stable joy, and genuine wholeness? Then let me show you the way.

I cannot promise you a perfect life. But I can promise you this — when you begin healing your body, mind, and spirit, the weight of sadness starts to lift. Reactivity softens. You gain awareness, regulation, and choice. Over time you learn how to respond instead of react, and how to live from your true self — the self Christ restores, not the one trauma created.

It takes time. It takes dedication. It is absolutely worth it.

Healer, Heal Thyself

God does not shame us into wholeness. He invites us into it. Healing is not a lack of faith — it is stewardship. God gives us insight through prayer, and He also gives us people, tools, and science to help our minds and bodies catch up to what the soul already knows.

You are not weak for needing help. You are wise for seeking it.

What follows are the modalities I personally used to heal my mind, body, and spirit. I share them not as prescriptions but as invitations — explore what resonates with you. If you need guidance, my contact information is at the end of this book.

Therapy

Therapy gave me a safe place to unpack what I had been carrying for years. Talking with a trained professional does not mean you lack faith — it means you value wholeness.

A good therapist helps you identify the thought patterns that keep you stuck, reframe painful experiences with clarity and compassion, and learn practical tools for anxiety, grief, and trauma. It reflects the way Jesus met people — listening without judgment, restoring dignity before offering direction. When you are truly seen and heard in a safe space, the nervous system relaxes. That is where healing begins.

I worked with therapists for twelve years. It changed my life completely.

Cognitive and Dialectical Skills

Our brains learn through repetition. Cognitive-behavioral therapy — CBT — teaches you to identify automatic negative thoughts and replace them with healthier, more balanced ones. Dialectical behavior therapy — DBT — builds emotional regulation, mindfulness, and distress tolerance. Together they teach you how to ride emotional waves instead of drowning in them.

These tools do not contradict faith. They support it. They help the brain learn what the soul already knows — that peace is possible.

Because of CBT and DBT, I learned how to interact with people more skillfully, how to catch destructive thoughts before they became destructive actions, and how to ask for what I needed clearly and calmly — in every kind of relationship. These skills transformed the way I showed up in my marriage, in my friendships, and in my work. A trained therapist can teach you the same.

Hypnotherapy

Hypnotherapy gently opens access to the subconscious mind — where old programming lives. In that deeply relaxed state, the inner script can be updated. Fear becomes safety. Shame becomes compassion. Old patterns that have run on autopilot for decades begin to release.

As a certified hypnotherapist, I use these techniques with my clients and with myself. If you feel called to explore this work, you are welcome to reach out and book a session with me.

Havening Techniques®

Havening combines soothing touch and guided visualization to help the brain release fear-based responses. It teaches the nervous system how to return to safety — gently, without force, without re-traumatization.

For most of my life, even after I found God, old shameful memories would surface without warning. I prayed. I tried to suppress them. Nothing worked — until I learned Havening. In just a few sessions, those memories stopped intruding. They lost their emotional charge. For the first time, I could think about my past without being pulled back into it.

That was real freedom.

You do not need to relive your trauma to heal it. If those intrusive memories are still haunting you, reach out. As a certified Havening Techniques Practitioner, I would love to walk through that healing with you.

Transcranial Magnetic Stimulation

For some people, depression runs deeper than talk therapy alone can reach. Transcranial magnetic stimulation — TMS — uses magnetic pulses to stimulate the areas of the brain involved in mood regulation. It is noninvasive, scientifically supported, and has helped many people when other approaches were not enough.

I personally completed six weeks of TMS treatment, and it made a significant difference in my life. Many insurance plans cover it, including VA benefits for veterans. Sometimes God's healing comes through medicine, technology, and research — and this can be one of those bridges.

Movement

Movement heals what words cannot reach. Exercise supports the brain, releases stored emotion, and builds confidence through consistency. When you move your body, you affirm life.

Let me be honest with you about where I started.

In 2016, after a serious car accident, I was walking with a cane and living in significant daily pain. I am only five feet tall, at that time my weight increased to 195 pounds and a size 18 in jeans. Alcohol, processed food, and self-neglect had become my coping mechanisms. I didn't move my body because I didn't love my body. And I didn't love my body because I hadn't yet learned to love myself.

Healing changed that. Slowly, with consistency and growing self-respect, my body followed my heart. Today I weigh 120 pounds and wear a size 3. I am strong, muscular, and fit — and I look younger now than I did back then.

I share that not to show off. I share it because I want you to see what is possible on the other side of healing. When we release our emotional baggage, our bodies often begin to heal alongside our hearts. And when we get active — when we move and breathe and build strength — the natural endorphins that follow make us genuinely happier in our everyday lives.

I am now a certified personal trainer, and I help women reclaim their strength and vitality. Confidence is built, not given. And your body is waiting to show you what it can do.

Spirit and Science Together

Some people look only to prayer. Others only to medicine. Wholeness lives in both.

Christ does not oppose science — He redeems it. Prayer aligns the heart. Therapy trains the mind. Medicine supports the body. Together they restore the harmony God always intended. Healing is not choosing between faith and science. It is receiving every gift God provides — and trusting that He is the source of all of them.

When mind, heart, spirit, and body align — life reorganizes itself around that alignment. That is not magic. That is coherence. That is what it looks like when a human being comes home to themselves.

And that homecoming is available to you.

Right now.

Exactly as you are.

A Moment for Reflection
No matter how broken, angry, or lost you feel right now, are you willing to believe that none of that is the final word on who you are?

Chapter 18
Healing Every Layer

*"If you bring forth what is within you,
what you bring forth will save you.
If you do not bring forth what is within you,
what you do not bring forth will destroy you."*
—The Gospel of Thomas, Saying 70

When you are ready to heal your life, understand this: God desires loving connection for you. From the very beginning of Scripture, we see Him drawing people into relationship — with Him and with one another. That desire has never changed.

Whether you are in a straight relationship or a same-sex partnership — whether you have been married for twenty years or are just beginning to build something new with someone — what follows is for you. God's design for love does not have a gender requirement. It has a foundation requirement. And that foundation is Him.

Are you in a relationship that feels broken? I know that pain. I have been there. Sometimes one of the hardest things we can do is let go of what *was* so that something healthier can emerge. But if you know in your heart that the person you are with is the one you want to be with — and you both desire to show up at your best — then let me share what I have learned as a certified relationship and spiritual coach.

And if you are single and longing to meet someone — keep reading. This is for you too.

Everyone deserves love. Everyone deserves a romantic union that is safe, life-giving, and enduring. The question is not whether you deserve it. The question is whether you are ready to build it.

Listen closely. Take notes.

Love Begins with the Source

Real love begins with God. If you try to pour love from an empty heart, you end up giving from need instead of overflow — and that is a recipe for pain on both sides. A spiritually grounded partnership begins when both people know God as their first love, and the relationship flows from that foundation — not the other way around.

Two whole people — not two wounded halves — come together and amplify the light already present in each other. A partner is a teammate. A collaborator. Someone who makes the word *we* feel like home.

Love is not something we chase. It is something we remember. And when we heal, we remember it more clearly.

Building Sacred Partnership

Every healthy relationship becomes a mirror — reflecting God back to us through the face of another person. When two people learn to love the way Jesus loved — patiently, kindly, without fear or domination — they create a living sanctuary where heaven touches earth.

This begins at home. No one in a partnership should feel like a servant. Share responsibility. Divide tasks fairly. Burnout and resentment grow quietly when one person carries the load alone — and by the time they speak up, the damage is often already done.

Women, do not shrink into becoming a maid in your own home. Be an equal. This is not about shaming your partner — it is about mutual respect. If you need support, say it plainly and kindly. Try something like this: *"Love, I cherish our partnership. I am feeling physically and emotionally exhausted trying to balance everything. Can we divide our responsibilities more evenly so we both can thrive?"*

And when your partner shows up — acknowledge it. Gratitude strengthens connection. Appreciation builds intimacy. Romance is not a destination — it is a daily practice.

If your partner consistently refuses to participate or justifies the imbalance, seek support. Talk with a therapist or relationship coach. Discern honestly whether healing is possible — or whether it is time to walk away. And remember this truth, which I want you to carry with you:

You don't get what you want. You get what you accept.

If someone repeatedly puts you down, harms you emotionally or physically, and you remain — that behavior is being permitted. You deserve better. Seek help. You are not failing by asking for support. You are choosing yourself.

A Living Example

With permission, I want to share the story of my dear friends Coral and Cory. Coral is a stay-at-home mom. Cory is the primary provider. I have known them for fourteen years. They have two beautiful boys. Coral manages the home because she *chooses* that role — it is not something that was imposed on her. And Cory works, but he also shows up — picking up the kids, playing with them, loving his wife, and modeling respect and presence every single day.

Their marriage is not perfect. But it is intentional. Every day, they choose each other.

Coral once told me, "Every day — on the good days and the hard ones — Cory and I choose each other. And we choose God in our marriage."

That is the difference. Not perfection. Intention. Choice. Over and over again.

What Are You Willing to Accept?

Ask yourself honestly — *what am I willing to tolerate in the name of love?*

Betrayal takes many forms. Infidelity is one of the deepest wounds. Emotional and physical abuse are never acceptable — not ever, not under any circumstance. Remaining in a harmful situation is not Christlike. It is self-abandonment.

I chose divorce after betrayal. I chose healing over denial. And I want you to know — honoring yourself is not a lack of faith. It is obedience to truth.

Be slow to give your heart and body. Get to know someone before committing deeply. Do not rush intimacy. Fire without foundation burns out quickly. When you are whole, you attract wholeness. Do the inner work, and love will meet you there.

Partnership with Purpose

"Two are better than one . . . and a threefold cord is not quickly broken."—Ecclesiastes 4:9–12

Every true partnership contains three presences — you, your partner, and God. When God is honored as the third strand, decisions become guided rather than forced. Arguments become conversations. Wounds become opportunities for healing rather than weapons for winning.

Communicate patiently. Stay calm. Speak truth without raising your voice. There is never a need for yelling, threats, or slammed doors. Those behaviors fracture trust — and when trust fractures, your partner begins to hide themselves from you, emotionally first and then physically. By the time you notice the distance, it has already been growing for a long time.

Here is a practical tool that transformed the way I communicate: use a simple object — a coin, a stone, anything small. Whoever holds it speaks. The other listens without interrupting. Then switch. It sounds simple because it is. And it works, because being truly heard is one of the deepest human needs there is.

When you speak about how you feel, always begin with *"I feel..."* — not *"You make me feel..."* The moment you say *you make me*, your partner hears blame and shuts down. When you say *I feel sad, hurt, or confused when this happens*, you open a door instead of closing one.

Strong, respectful communication keeps love alive. And intimacy — real intimacy, the kind that is rooted in safety and not performance — flourishes when conflict is handled with grace.

Healing Together

Couples who heal together grow together. Invite your partner into reflection, movement, laughter, and service. Flirt. Play. Stay genuinely curious about who your partner is becoming — because people grow, and love must grow with them.

Romance does not fade from age. It fades from neglect. So behave as though you are meeting your partner for the first time. Choose them again today. And tomorrow. And the day after that.

The Fruits of Sacred Love

When love matures in the way of Christ, something beautiful begins to appear. Peace that weathers storms becomes the ground you stand on. Intimacy rooted in safety replaces the kind that feeds on anxiety. Communication becomes clear and honest rather than a guessing game. Shared joy soothes what stress has tightened. And purpose — the sense that your love exists not just for the two of you but for something greater — begins to extend outward into service, into community, into the world.

This kind of love is not possessed. It is witnessed. It is the love Jesus modeled — healing, forgiving, protecting, enduring — and it is the love we are invited to embody in our own lives and our own homes.

It is not a fantasy. It is a practice.

And it begins the moment you decide you are worth it.

> **A Moment for Reflection**
> Are you ready to look honestly at every layer of your life — spiritual, emotional, and relational — and allow healing to begin from the inside out?

Chapter 19
Building Sacred Partnership

"Come to me, all you who are weary and burdened,
and I will give you rest. Take my yoke upon you and
learn from me, for I am gentle and humble in heart,
and you will find rest for your souls.
For my yoke is easy and my burden is light."
—Matthew 11:28–30 (NIV)

Today I live in the loving arms of Christ consciousness. And when you embody Christ, this is how you will feel too.

Right now — not someday, not after you have it all figured out — you have 100 percent access to God. All day. Every day. Blessings flow to you with ease and grace when you simply surrender and receive them. Joy overflows. Inner peace stays with you. Depression fades. Shame loosens its grip. Fear no longer rules you.

That is not a promise for a perfect life. It is a promise for a different way of carrying this one.

A yoke was a wooden beam used to link two oxen so they could share the load. When Jesus invites us to take His yoke, He is saying — *walk beside me. Let's carry this together.* That is the heart of everything. Surrender is not weakness. It is the wisest thing you can do.

As love takes root in you, something remarkable happens. You look and feel younger because your body responds to peace. You become comfortable in your own skin. You fall in love with who you are. Old habits begin to fall away. Substances lose their appeal.

You naturally move toward people and environments that feel life-giving — not because you are forcing it, but because you are finally aligned with what God always intended for you.

Manifesting Heaven on Earth

"Thy kingdom come. Thy will be done in earth, as it is in heaven." — Matthew 6:10 (KJV)

The language of manifestation is modern, but the principle runs throughout Scripture. Faith, words, and alignment with God bring the unseen into form. Jesus demonstrated this through healing, provision, and restoration — again and again.

If you are asking God to bring you a love or partner, here is where to begin.

Stand in front of a mirror and ask yourself honestly — *"Would I marry someone like me?"* If the answer is yes, you are ready. If the answer brings hesitation or fear, that is not failure. That is clarity. Healing comes first. Always.

Heal your past. Heal your mind. Heal your body. Heal your soul. I have shared what worked for me — now take action for yourself. Practice self-respect, self-care, and compassion — including in the way you speak to yourself. The words you say to yourself in private are shaping your life in ways you may not yet see.

As you heal, prepare your environment for love. Love is energy, and energy responds to space. Bring beauty into your home. Place images that reflect partnership and romance — two people sharing a moment, hearts on the wall, something that reminds you daily of what you are believing for. Write down what you desire — not to control it, but to clarify it. Describe the kind of partner you want to grow with.

Then live your life. Go out. Be present. Make connections without pressure. Don't chase — *be* love in action. Be friendly. Smile. Stay curious about people. When you stop forcing outcomes, energy softens and doors open naturally.

Ask, Believe, Receive

"Ask, and it shall be given you; seek, and ye shall find; knock, and it shall be opened unto you." —Matthew 7:7–8 (KJV)

Speak your prayers out loud. Be specific. Imagine yourself already living the life you are praying for — and then relax into that feeling.

When I pray for something I desire, I do it three ways. I prophesy it. I declare it. And I thank God for it.

It sounds like this: *"God, I prophesy and declare that I will meet my future partner this year. I declare this in heaven. Thank you, God, for hearing my prayer."*

Then I get up and do my part. Faith without action is dead — so keep your prayers alive by moving toward the life you are believing for. Pray boldly. Work consistently. Trust completely.

Words Carry Creative Power

"For by thy words thou shalt be justified, and by thy words thou shalt be condemned." —Matthew 12:36–37 (KJV)

Words shape reality. Be mindful of what you speak — to others and to yourself. When a negative thought surfaces, interrupt it immediately. Cancel it and replace it with truth. This is where inner work, prayer, and healing practices rewire the mind over time — thought by thought, day by day.

Gratitude Multiplies Everything

"And Jesus took the loaves, and when he had given thanks . . ."—John 6:11 (KJV)

Before every miracle, Jesus gave thanks. Not after — before. Gratitude is not a response to blessing. It is the posture that invites it.

Thank God daily — for what you have, for what is coming, and for what you cannot yet see. Gratitude keeps your heart open and aligned. It is faith made visible.

Jesus showed us how heaven touches earth: faith spoken, gratitude expressed, trust embodied, and grace released.

That is manifestation in its purest and most powerful form.

And it is available to you — right now, exactly as you are, right where you stand.

> **A Moment for Reflection**
> What would your relationships look like if you surrendered control and chose instead to walk alongside others in the gentleness and grace of love?

Chapter 20

Following God's Voice Within

"But he answered and said, It is written,
Man shall not live by bread alone, but by every word
that proceedeth out of the mouth of God."
—Matthew 4:4 (KJV)

What has God taught me?

He has taught me that when I surrender to His love, grace, and mercy, I am protected, guided, loved, blessed, and anointed. Every single time. Not sometimes. Every time.

I think often about Jesus in the desert — alone, fasting, hungry, facing the full weight of temptation. The adversary came to Him at His weakest moment and whispered, *"If you are the Son of God, command these stones to become bread."* And Jesus answered not with argument, not with anger, but with truth: *Man shall not live by bread alone, but by every word that proceedeth out of the mouth of God.*

That answer changed everything I understood about hunger — and about where real nourishment comes from.

The Inner Word

Bread represents everything we reach for to keep ourselves feeling secure — money, approval, comfort, control, validation. The things we grasp for when the world feels unstable and we need something solid to hold. Jesus was not telling us those things don't matter. He was telling us they are not enough. They cannot sustain the soul. Our deepest hunger is not for success or survival — it is for communion with God.

He was pointing to the living voice of God — the guidance, conviction, wisdom, and inspiration that flows through the soul when the heart is surrendered. Scripture points us toward that voice and anchors us in truth, while the Spirit brings it to life within us. Together they become the daily bread the soul cannot live without.

I know this from experience. There were years when I reached for everything except God — substances, relationships, work, distraction — trying to fill a hunger that none of those things were designed to satisfy. It was only when I stopped reaching outward and started listening inward that the hunger began to ease. Not because my circumstances changed immediately, but because I had finally found the source.

God Speaks — Inside and Out

God speaks in more ways than most of us realize.

He speaks internally — through conscience, through insight, through spiritual awareness, through the quiet inner prompting that draws us toward peace, humility, and love. You will know it is His voice by its fruit. It is never frantic. It is never condemning. It is never prideful. It leads toward love, patience, humility, peace, and clarity. If what you hear pulls you away from those things, pause — that is not God's voice.

He speaks externally too — through Scripture, through people, through nature, through circumstance, and even through challenges that reveal what still needs healing or growth. A billboard on a Denver freeway. A stranger on a road trip who says the same thing everyone else has been saying. A card that flies out of a deck. God is not confined to the expected.

When both of these — the internal and the external — are recognized and held together, life becomes a conversation with God. When I learned to listen inwardly while remaining grounded in Christ, I stopped chasing fulfillment outside myself. God became both the air around me and the breath within me.

Recognizing the Voice

The voice of God is not dramatic. It does not shout. It does not shame. It is the gentle prompting that arises within awareness and leads toward Christlike action. It is the quiet knowing that says *wait, forgive, speak,* or *be still.* It is compassion that appears before the mind can reason it away. It is comfort that arrives without explanation, reminding you that you are not alone.

Jesus told us we would know truth by its fruit — and this is how I test what I hear. God's voice produces love, patience, humility, peace, self-control, and clarity. It forms you rather than flatters you. It asks things of you rather than simply telling you what you want to hear.

If you are unsure whether what you are hearing is God — ask yourself: does this lead me toward love and humility, or toward ego and fear? That question alone will give you more clarity than you expect.

A Daily Practice: Listening for the Living Word

Learning to hear God's voice is not complicated — but it does require consistency and a willingness to be still. Here is the practice that transformed my relationship with Him.

Begin by sitting quietly for a few minutes and breathing until your thoughts settle. The noise of the day needs somewhere to go before you can hear what is underneath it. Then, with an open heart, silently invite His presence: *"Speak, Lord. I am listening."*

Then simply feel — don't force. Notice what arises gently. Thoughts, impressions, emotions that carry peace rather than pressure. God rarely speaks in urgency. He speaks in stillness.

Write down or record what you sense — without editing, without judging. I often record my prayers and reflections so I can notice patterns over time. When you look back over weeks and months, you begin to see how consistently God has been speaking, even in the moments you thought He was silent.

Finally, always test the fruit. Ask yourself — does this guidance produce love, humility, peace, patience, and alignment with Christ? If yes, trust it. If not, pause and seek further discernment through prayer and Scripture. God's voice will always confirm itself through love.

The more you practice this, the clearer His guidance becomes. Listening is only the beginning. Trust grows through obedience, humility, and time. This is how faith becomes movement — and how the Word within becomes the path beneath your feet.

Scripture, Spirit, and Relationship

"I can do all things through Christ which strengtheneth me." — Philippians 4:13 (KJV)

At the beginning of this book, I shared that I first came to Scripture through research — not devotion. That is the truth. I did not grow up reading the Bible. I came to it sideways, through questions, through conversations with God, through a burning need to understand what He was showing me.

Today, I experience Scripture as living testimony — words that point me back to God every time I open them. Texts like the Ethiopian Bible and the Nag Hammadi Library have offered me historical and spiritual perspectives that deepened my understanding. But Christ remains my compass. Always.

When God breathed His Holy Spirit into me in that shower in 2017, He did not just give me an experience. He initiated a lifelong relationship. He teaches me. He corrects me. He disciplines me when I need it — as He did in that Colorado Springs cabin with the lighter and the candle. He comforts me. He protects me. He guides me.

My relationship with God is not a system or a theology. It is active, personal, and alive — grounded in Christ and growing every single day.

And that same relationship is available to you.

Not someday. Not after you have cleaned up your life or figured everything out or become someone different than you are right now.

Now.

Go within. He is already there — waiting, patient, and deeply in love with you.

"Seek, and ye shall find." (Matthew 7:7, KJV)

He means it. He has always meant it.

Go find Him.

> **A Moment for Reflection**
> What are you reaching for — approval, comfort, security — that is keeping you from going inward and being nourished by the voice of God already within you?

Chapter 21
Your Call to Awakening

Whether you are queer or straight, religious or not, addicted or in recovery, broken by betrayal or by loss or by love — if you made it to these final pages, this chapter is yours. You did not find this book by accident. You were led here. And what I want you to know before you read another word is this — everything that follows is written for you. Not for a category of person. Not for a specific community. For you. Exactly as you are. Exactly where you are. Right now.

Dear Friend,

If you are reading these words, you have traveled through time with me — from darkness to light. You have witnessed a life nearly destroyed by trauma, addiction, and shame, and you have seen that same life transformed by God's unconditional love.

What you have read is not just my story. It may feel like a mirror. It may feel like an invitation — to gently look at your own life with compassion and honesty, and to ask yourself what is still waiting to be healed, released, or remembered.

I am so glad you made it to these last pages. And I mean that with my whole heart.

You Are Not Your Past

You are not the trauma you have experienced. You are not the addiction you have struggled with. You are not the version of yourself that acted out of pain, fear, or survival. And the shame that religious people may have placed on you? That was never God's truth about you. It was never the truth at all.

What you truly are is a living expression of God, experiencing life through your unique and irreplaceable soul. The Christ within you waits patiently — not to judge, but to remind you of who you are.

You are Divine Love. You have always been Divine Love.

An Invitation

I am not asking you to join a religion or even call yourself a Christian. I am not asking you to follow a set of rules or perform a version of faith that does not feel true to you. I am simply inviting you to listen again — to the voice of Love that has always been within you. To consider the possibility that you and God are not separated by distance or failure or the weight of everything you have done or left undone — but are already held together in grace.

That grace has been there the whole time. It was there in your darkest moment. It is here now.

A Word for Those Who Feel It Is Too Late

If you believe your past disqualifies you from God's love — please hear this clearly: it does not. Nothing you have done, nothing you have been, nothing you have survived places you beyond His reach. Healing begins with willingness, not perfection. You do not need to have it together to come to God. You just need to come.

A Word for the LGBTQ Community

If faith communities made you feel rejected, condemned, or less than — I am truly sorry. On behalf of every person who used God's name to wound you, I am sorry. You are not broken. You are not an accident. You are not a mistake. You are fully and completely loved by God exactly as He made you. Nothing about who you are separates you from His presence. Nothing ever has.

Healing from Religious Trauma

If religion hurt you, please do not confuse that with God. Jesus did not weaponize love. He welcomed the wounded, the rejected, the misunderstood, and the outcast. He saved His harshest words not for sinners — but for the religious leaders who used their power to exclude and condemn. Love was always the point. It is still the point today.

A Promise

If you choose this path — slowly, honestly, imperfectly — your life may begin to feel different. Not easier, necessarily. But truer. Pain may still visit, but it will no longer define you. Love will have more room to move. And you will find, as I did, that God was never far away. He was simply waiting — as He always does — for you to turn toward Him.

This is where our written journey ends. Your real journey continues — quietly, uniquely, beautifully — in your own life. You already have what you need. The wisdom is within you. God is with you. Take the next step when you are ready.

With love and deep faith in who you are becoming,
Fenix

Epilogue

To every reader who has loved someone they could not have —

You are not foolish for loving deeply. You are not weak for holding on longer than you should have. And you are not broken because it did not work out the way you hoped.

You are human. And you are loved — by a God who knows exactly how you feel, because He has felt it too. He has reached toward people who turned away. He has loved without guarantee of return. He has held open hands for longer than any of us can comprehend.

You were not wrong to love.

You were just loving the way God loves.

And that love — patient, pure, and unconditional — is never wasted. It goes somewhere. It does something. It changes you into someone more capable of love than you were before.

That is the gift hidden inside every heartbreak.

Keep your heart open. Keep walking forward. Keep loving people where they are.

And trust God with everything you cannot control.

God has never stopped loving you. Not once.

With love,
Fenix

Afterword
The Way Shower

If what you have read in this book has resonated with you, I want you to know this first — you are not alone. What God has done in my life, He desires to do in yours as well. Gently, personally, and in His perfect timing.

I offer online masterclasses, live workshops, and spaces for prayer, reflection, and healing. If you ever feel led to join one, I would love to meet you, to pray with you, and to walk alongside you for a season. To me, you are not a client. You are a sister or brother in Christ.

As The Unconventional Counselor, I work with people who are ready to heal wounds from the past. If you are carrying shame, religious trauma, the aftermath of assault, or memories that still weigh heavily on your heart — you do not have to carry them alone. Together, we invite God into the healing process, allowing Him to loosen what has been stuck and bring peace where pain once lived. I use therapeutic tools such as Havening Techniques® and hypnotherapy as supports — never replacements — for God's restoring work.

I am also a certified relationship and spiritual coach and a nationally and state-certified peer support specialist. If you and your partner sense that something has been lost along the way — connection, intimacy, or understanding — I would be honored to help guide you back to remembering the love that first brought you together.

If you have been hurt by religion — by Christianity, Catholicism, or any belief system that used fear instead of love — I see you. If you desire a relationship with God that feels safe, compassionate, and real, I will walk with you as you rediscover the way of Christ within. I call God "Abba" because that is how I have come to know Him — close, loving, and faithful.

Above all, know this: I am here to serve, not to stand above you. I am a humble servant of God — still learning, still growing, still listening. My prayer for you is simple. That you are healed. That you are filled with peace. That you remember how brightly your light shines.

Jesus taught us not to hide that light — but to let it shine so that others may see love made visible in a human life.

May God bless you and keep you. May love guide your steps. May peace rest in your heart.

You are love. You are light. You belong to God.

Now go — and let your life shine.

With love,
Fenix

Meet Fenix

At fourteen, Fenix Shepard left home with nothing but wounds no child should carry, and a God she had already been told would never accept her—because she was born gay.

What followed was not a stumble. It was a freefall. Drug abuse. Sexual abuse. Self-harm. A loneliness so deep it had no bottom. She looked for love in every broken place she could find and came up empty every time.

Then one night, out of options and out of hope, she asked God the questions she had been terrified to ask. *Why am I so sick? Why did you make me gay just to condemn me? Why don't you love me?*

She expected silence. She got something else entirely.

God did not send her to a church. He came to her. Personally. Relentlessly. And what He showed her dismantled everything she had ever been told about who deserves to be loved.

Today, Fenix is an author, spiritual practitioner, and founder of The Unconventional Counselor—walking alongside the ones who have been told the same lies she was. The unseen. The shamed. The ones who gave up on God because God's people gave up on them first.

Loved Unconditionally is her testimony. And a reminder that no one—not even you—is too far gone.

Dear Reader,

I'm so glad you made it this far, and I want to thank you from the bottom of my heart for reading *Loved Unconditionally*. It means more to me than I can fully express.

If something in this book touched your heart, encouraged you, or helped you feel seen, I gently ask that you consider leaving a review wherever you purchased the book. Your words may help someone else find this story and be touched by God's love as you have been.

And if you feel ready to go deeper, to continue your journey of self-discovery and build a more personal relationship with God, I would be honored to walk alongside you. You are welcome to explore working with me at FenixShepard.com.

With love and gratitude,
Fenix

Ways to Work Together

One-on-One Coaching — If you are ready to heal trauma, release shame, and step into the fullness of who God created you to be, I would love to walk alongside you personally.

Relationship Coaching — If your relationship feels broken or disconnected, we work together to rebuild trust, deepen intimacy, and restore the foundation of love that brought you together.

The Phoenix Way Masterclass — A group healing experience for those ready to awaken holistically — spiritually, emotionally, and relationally. Community, coaching, and Christ consciousness — all in one space.

Speaking and Workshops — I speak at events, conferences, churches, and organizations on mental health, healing, spiritual awakening, and addiction and recovery. If you would like to bring this message to your community, I would be honored.

Book Fenix to Speak

Fenix Shepard is an award-winning public speaker with a passion for mental health, healing, spiritual transformation, and addiction recovery. To book Fenix for your event or podcast, contact her at Connect@FenixShepard.com.

Wedding Officiant

Fenix believes deeply in the sanctity of marriage and would be honored to officiate your wedding. As Reverend Fenix Shepard, she will help you create a ceremony that reflects the love, faith, and sacred union between you and your partner. Reach out at Connect@FenixShepard.com to begin the conversation.

www.ingramcontent.com/pod-product-compliance
Lightning Source LLC
Chambersburg PA
CBHW071512140726
47997CB00005B/1951